W9-BNI-331

STAR WARS™

ORIGAMI

11 Amazing Paper-folding Projects from a Galaxy Far, Far Away....

CHARACTERS

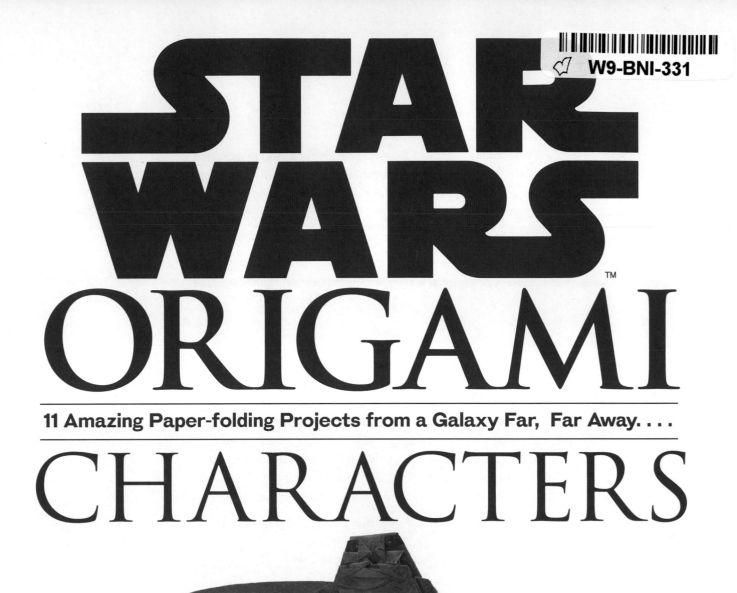

CHRIS ALEXANDER

WORKMAN PUBLISHING ✹ NEW YORK

Copyright © 2016 by Lucasfilm Ltd. & © or ™ where indicated.
Title and character and place names protected by all applicable trademark laws.
All Rights Reserved. Used Under Authorization.

All rights reserved. No portion of this book may be reproduced—mechanically, electronically,
or by any other means, including photocopying—without written permission of the publisher.
Published simultaneously in Canada by Thomas Allen & Son Limited.

Library of Congress Cataloging-in-Publication Data is available.

978-0-7611-9102-5

Design by Netta Rabin
Package design by Abby Dening

Origami paper illustrations by Phil Conigliaro
Origami designs, diagrams, and text by Chris Alexander

Workman books are available at special discounts when purchased in bulk for
premiums and sales promotions as well as for fund-raising or educational use.
Special editions or book excerpts can also be created to specification.
For details, contact the Special Sales Director at the address below,
or send an email to specialmarkets@workman.com.

Workman Publishing Company, Inc.
225 Varick Street
New York, NY 10014-4381
workman.com
starwars.com

WORKMAN is a registered trademark of Workman Publishing Co., Inc.

Printed in China
First printing March 2016

10 9 8 7 6 5 4 3 2 1

FOR MY MOM, JAN

A truly luminous being

ACKNOWLEDGMENTS

I'd like to take this time to thank several people who have had a lot to do with this book becoming a reality: First and foremost, Jan Alexander, who started me down the origami path when I was just four years old. Colleen O'Rourke, Fran Siller, and Ira Nixon: Without their love, friendship, and support through the years I would have long ago given up any hope that the book would ever be published. Chris Colquhoun, who, fifteen years ago, planted the seed that was to become this book. Tom Purpus and the numerous volunteers who've joined me at *Star Wars* events to teach my origami to the public. Origami masters Robert Lang and Michael La Fosse, for their encouragement. Tom Angleberger and Troy Alders, for putting the buzz in the right ears.

The hardworking talent at Workman Publishing, especially Raquel Jaramillo, Krestyna Lypen, Phil Conigliaro, Netta Rabin, and Beth Levy, for taking that buzz and making it a reality.

And of course, Mr. George Lucas, without whom the galaxy far, far away would never have existed.

CONTENTS

A LONG TIME AGO IN A GALAXY FAR, FAR AWAY. . . .

WITH THESE WORDS, *STAR WARS,* A SAGA of epic proportions, was born. First appearing in movie theaters on May 25, 1977, it had all the elements of a timeless myth: heroes, villains, monsters, knights, a princess in distress, and a climactic battle of good and evil.

Of course, the *Star Wars* universe also captivated audiences with its extraordinary aliens, droids, creatures, vehicles, and starships. Their distinctive shapes from long ago and far away are perfectly suited for re-creation in the present through the ancient art of origami. And so, a little bit of time ago, in a town in California that is not so far away, the concept for this book was born.

Origami can be defined as the Japanese art of sculpting by folding a piece of paper. Its exact origins are unknown, but it probably dates back to A.D. 600, when a Buddhist priest introduced Chinese paper-making methods to Japan. The Japanese saw the potential for shapes and forms in the paper. Throughout the ensuing centuries, the Japanese learned how to re-create the birds and animals around them, turning paper folding into an art form.

The purest form of origami starts with a single square of paper. Tearing the sheet, taping pieces together, or using tools to help the folding process are not allowed. Some artists, however, believe that as long as the paper is folded it can begin as any shape; you can cut the paper, glue it, or even combine multiple pieces of paper. My opinion is somewhere in the middle. I prefer not to glue the paper, but the number of pieces and starting shape are irrelevant, as long as it's within reason. As you explore this ancient art form and encounter the incredible variety of figures that can be made from a simple piece of paper, you can make your own decisions.

This book contains instructions for re-creating eleven characters from the *Star Wars* universe with just a simple piece of paper (or two). Though you can do the projects in any order you choose, there are four levels of difficulty: Youngling, Padawan, Jedi Knight, and Jedi Master. Unless you're already an origami guru, you might want to start with the Youngling or Padawan models first.

The diagrams in this book are designed to help you visualize the steps, and because of this, some of the edges are offset. Do not take these literally. By making all of your creases as accurate as possible, your model will be easier to fold and look neater when finished.

For example, in the center diagram to the right, the edges do not meet in the middle. But when properly folded there will be a sharp point at the top, and the edges will line up perfectly.

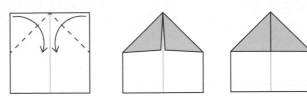

A typical diagram   *What your paper should look like*

When making a fold, glance ahead to the next step to see what it should look like when completed. It is very important to line up each fold as accurately as you can, especially in the earlier stages of the model. Try to start the crease right at a corner or point, and line up the edges along another edge or crease. Once you have the fold lined up, be sure to crease the paper sharply by running your fingernail along it a few times. This makes the crease more accurate, and the next step easier.

One last note: While origami is an art form, it is a simple and inexpensive art form. Any type of paper can be used, and it can be done anywhere. Like anything else, practice makes perfect. If in the beginning your models are not coming out the way they should, don't worry. Crumple it up, tell everyone it's a piece of the exploded Death Star, and try again.

Happy folding!

PART ONE
THE BASICS

ORIGAMI DEFINITIONS, SYMBOLS, AND BASIC FOLDS

Origami figures are made with just two folds, the valley fold and the mountain fold. All of the following folds are just combinations of these. As you study the diagrams, pay attention to the type of line used to represent each crease. This will indicate whether it should be a mountain or valley fold.

SIDE ONE

Side one of the origami paper is represented by the white side of the diagram.

SIDE TWO

Side two of the origami paper is represented by the colored side of the diagram.

START ARROW

This symbol, printed on the origami paper in the back of the book, tells you which way to orient the paper. The arrow should always point straight up.

VALLEY FOLD - - - - - - - - - - - - - - - -

The valley fold, represented by a dashed line, is the most common fold. The paper is creased along the line as one side is folded toward you. A "valley" is formed in the process.

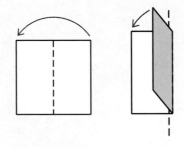

MOUNTAIN FOLD · — · · — · · — · · — · · —

The mountain fold is represented by a dashed and dotted line. The paper is creased along the line as one side is folded away from you. A "mountain" is formed as the paper is folded.

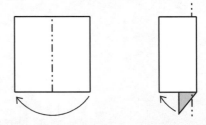

MARK FOLD

The mark fold is used to make a crease that will be used as a reference in a later step. Lightly fold on the line as indicated and then unfold. Ideally, the crease will not be visible when the model is finished.

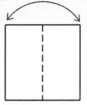

EXISTING CREASE

A thin line represents a crease formed in a previous step and is used for orientation or as a reference in the current step.

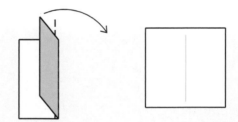

X-RAY LINES

The dotted line serves two purposes. In most cases it represents a fold or edge underneath another layer of paper. It is also used to represent an imaginary extension of an existing line.

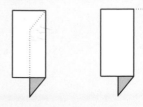

TURN OVER

This symbol means turn the model over to the other side.

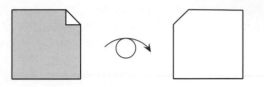

ROTATE

This symbol means rotate the figure to a new position.

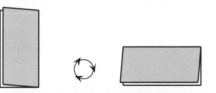

CUT

This symbol means you should cut the paper along the indicated solid line.

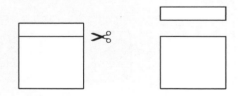

REVERSE FOLD

To make a reverse fold (sometimes called an inside reverse fold) put your finger inside the pocket to spread it open. Then, push down on the spine of the section to be reversed until the section is folded inside itself along existing creases.

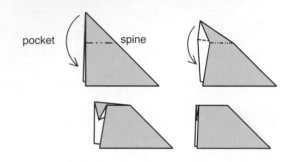

PIVOT FOLD

The pivot fold adjusts an existing point. The base of the figure is pinched while the point is swiveled into its new location and is re-creased. In this example, pinch point A, while pivoting point B upward.

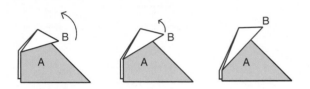

Start with an outside reverse fold.

OUTSIDE REVERSE FOLD

To make an outside reverse fold, open the pocket a bit and flip the point backward over the spine along existing creases. It's a little like peeling a banana.

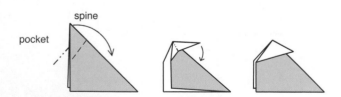

HOW TO MAKE A SQUARE

The only thing you will need to create an origami model is a square piece of paper. Specially designed origami paper is provided at the end of this book, and you can purchase origami paper in craft stores, online, and in some bookstores. But if you want to practice your techniques, this is a simple way to create your own origami paper! A square can be made out of any rectangle by following these steps.

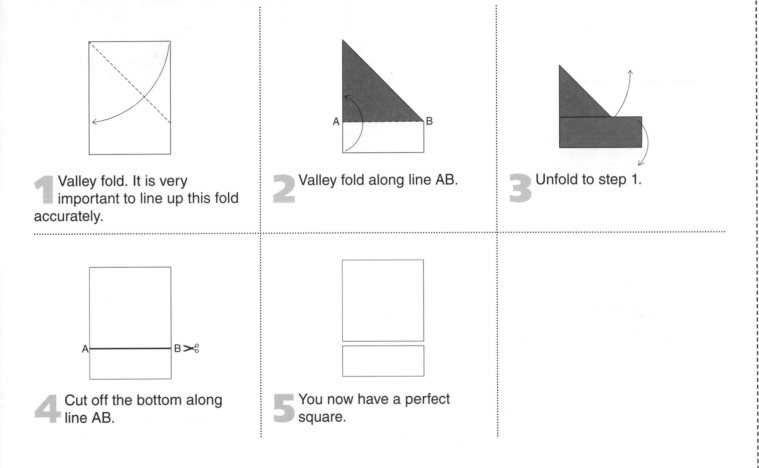

1 Valley fold. It is very important to line up this fold accurately.

2 Valley fold along line AB.

3 Unfold to step 1.

4 Cut off the bottom along line AB.

5 You now have a perfect square.

HOW TO MAKE AN EQUILATERAL TRIANGLE

An equilateral triangle has 60-degree angles at each of its corners, and has sides that are exactly the same length. Lucky for us, origami is based on geometric concepts. You won't need a protractor or ruler to map out the shape. This special triangle can be made from any rectangular or square piece of paper. Simply follow these steps.

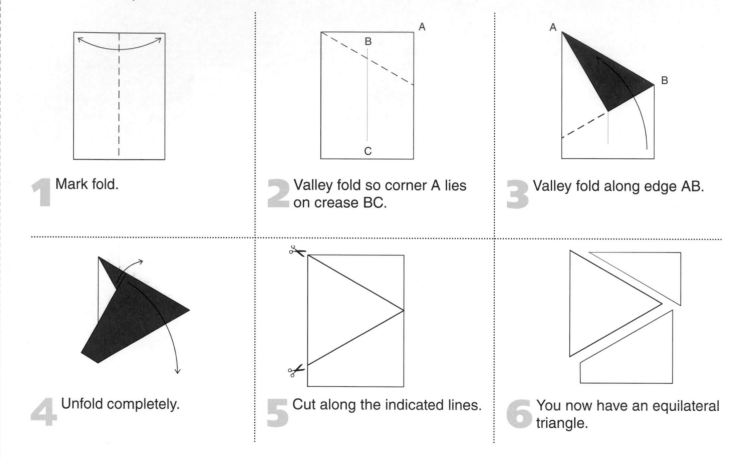

1 Mark fold.

2 Valley fold so corner A lies on crease BC.

3 Valley fold along edge AB.

4 Unfold completely.

5 Cut along the indicated lines.

6 You now have an equilateral triangle.

PLEAT FOLD

This fold resembles the pleat on a skirt when finished. You can think of it as two reverse folds.

This arrow indicates a pleat fold:

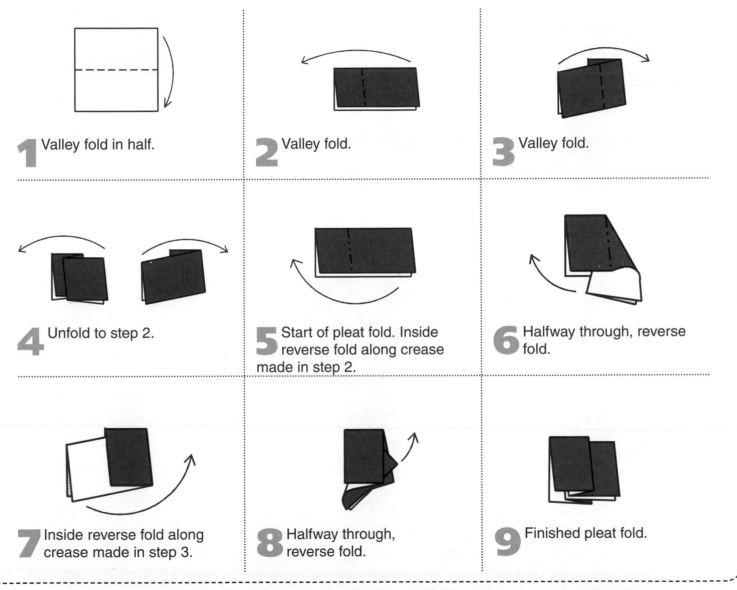

1 Valley fold in half.

2 Valley fold.

3 Valley fold.

4 Unfold to step 2.

5 Start of pleat fold. Inside reverse fold along crease made in step 2.

6 Halfway through, reverse fold.

7 Inside reverse fold along crease made in step 3.

8 Halfway through, reverse fold.

9 Finished pleat fold.

RABBIT EAR FOLD

This fold is used to narrow a point. In this example, the bottom half of the two existing creases are used, and two new creases are formed: the valley fold from the point to the center and the mountain fold from the center to the edge.

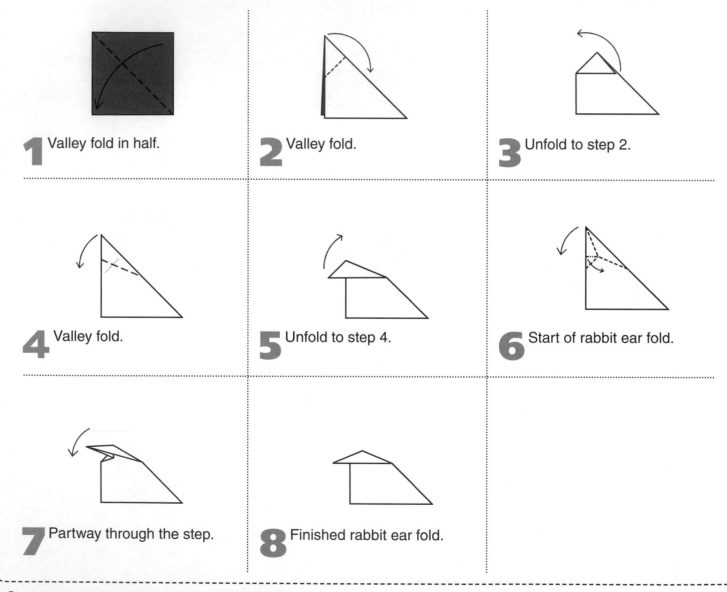

1 Valley fold in half.

2 Valley fold.

3 Unfold to step 2.

4 Valley fold.

5 Unfold to step 4.

6 Start of rabbit ear fold.

7 Partway through the step.

8 Finished rabbit ear fold.

SQUASH FOLD

A squash fold is formed by lifting one edge of a pocket and reforming it so the edge becomes a crease and an existing crease becomes a new edge.

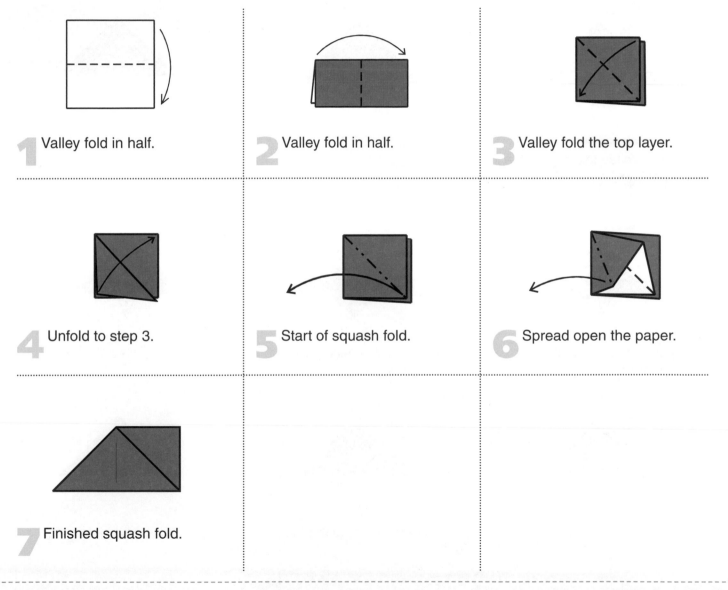

1 Valley fold in half.

2 Valley fold in half.

3 Valley fold the top layer.

4 Unfold to step 3.

5 Start of squash fold.

6 Spread open the paper.

7 Finished squash fold.

PETAL FOLD

Petal folds are used to isolate a point. This example starts with a waterbomb base (see p. 15). As the point is lifted, two new valley folds are added at the bottom.

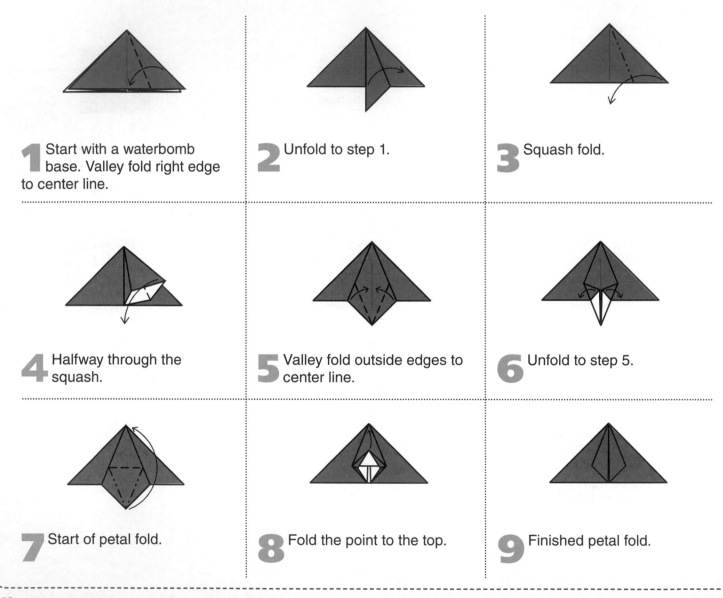

1 Start with a waterbomb base. Valley fold right edge to center line.

2 Unfold to step 1.

3 Squash fold.

4 Halfway through the squash.

5 Valley fold outside edges to center line.

6 Unfold to step 5.

7 Start of petal fold.

8 Fold the point to the top.

9 Finished petal fold.

SINK FOLD EXAMPLE 1

A sink fold requires unfolding a portion of the model. The section to be sunk is pushed inside-out along existing creases, and the model is then re-formed. No new creases are added. This arrow indicates a sink fold: **⌄**

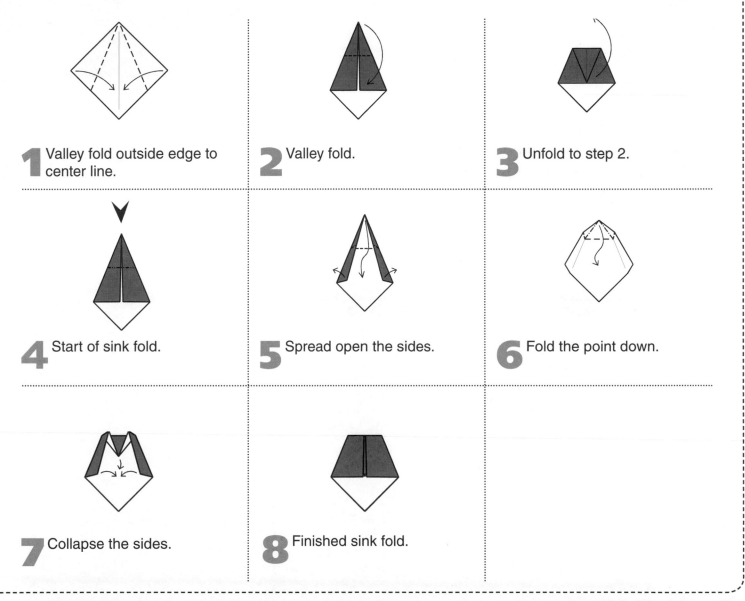

1 Valley fold outside edge to center line.

2 Valley fold.

3 Unfold to step 2.

4 Start of sink fold.

5 Spread open the sides.

6 Fold the point down.

7 Collapse the sides.

8 Finished sink fold.

SINK FOLD EXAMPLE 2

This example of a sink fold starts with a waterbomb base (see p. 15).

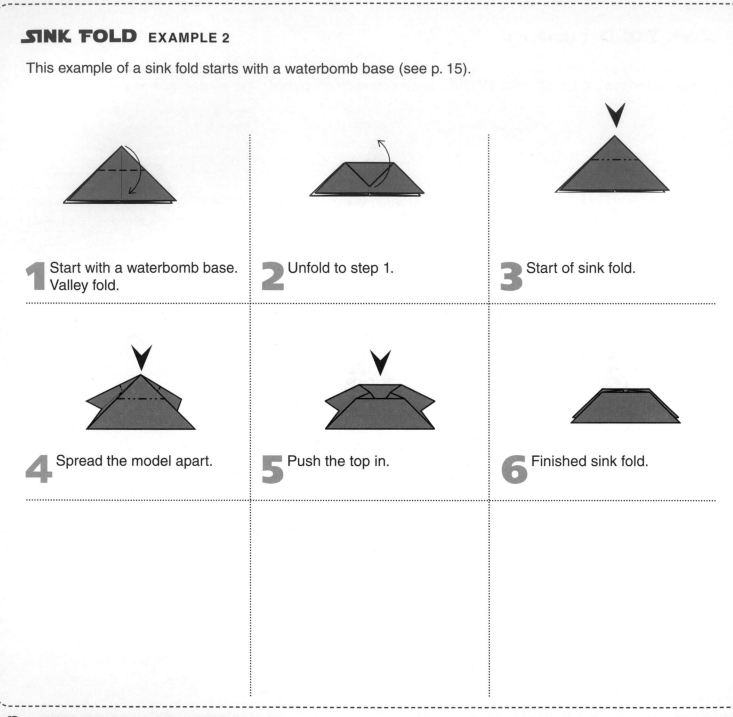

1 Start with a waterbomb base. Valley fold.

2 Unfold to step 1.

3 Start of sink fold.

4 Spread the model apart.

5 Push the top in.

6 Finished sink fold.

IMPORTANT ORIGAMI BASES

THE PRELIMINARY BASE

Bases are the building blocks of origami. The preliminary base is used as a starting point for many origami models.

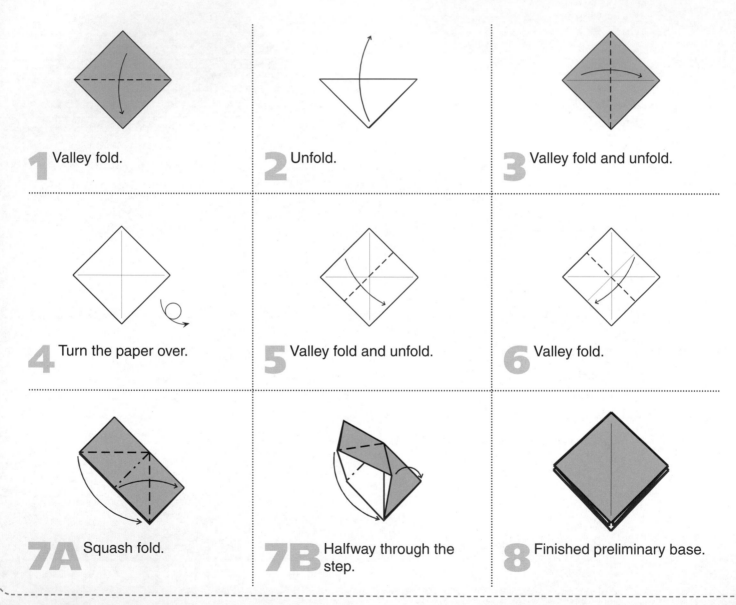

1 Valley fold.

2 Unfold.

3 Valley fold and unfold.

4 Turn the paper over.

5 Valley fold and unfold.

6 Valley fold.

7A Squash fold.

7B Halfway through the step.

8 Finished preliminary base.

THE WATERBOMB BASE

The waterbomb base is another common starting point for many origami models.

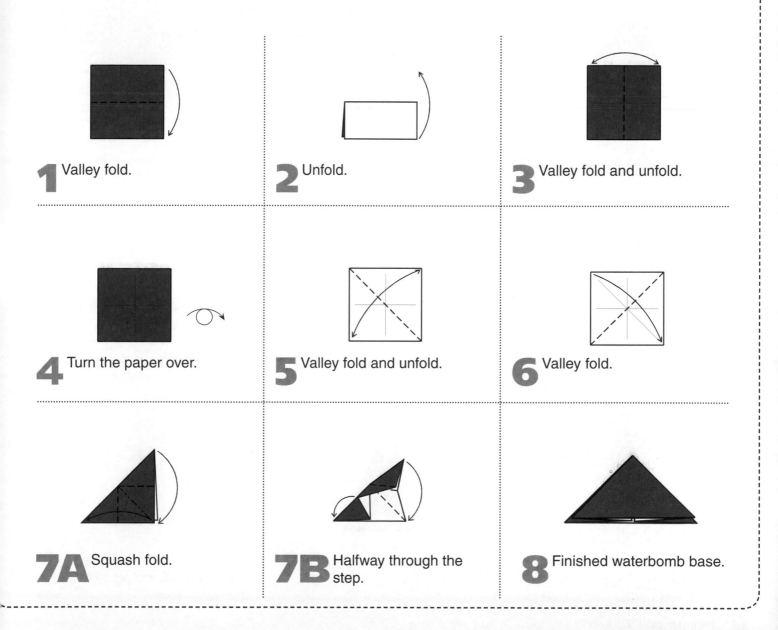

1 Valley fold.

2 Unfold.

3 Valley fold and unfold.

4 Turn the paper over.

5 Valley fold and unfold.

6 Valley fold.

7A Squash fold.

7B Halfway through the step.

8 Finished waterbomb base.

DISPLAY STAND

This little stand can be used to show off your origami models. Start with a piece of paper about a fourth of the size that you used for the model. Steps 9 through 13 can be adjusted to position the model to your liking.

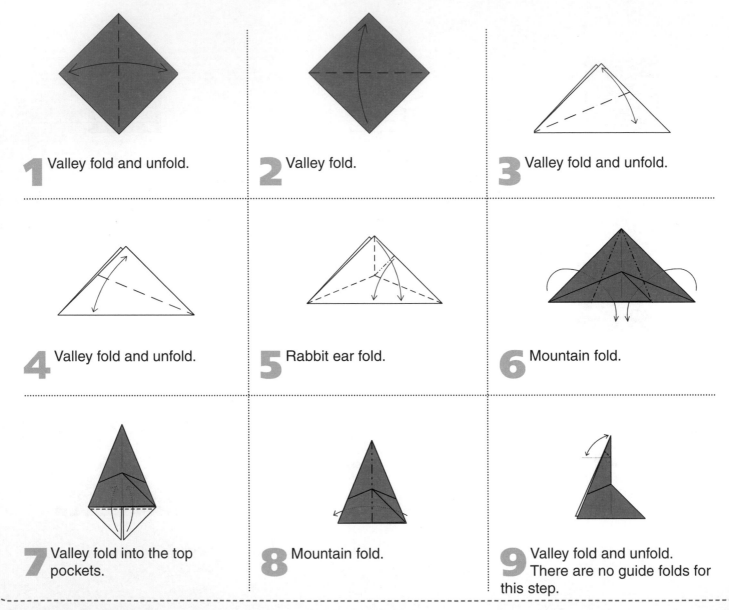

1 Valley fold and unfold.

2 Valley fold.

3 Valley fold and unfold.

4 Valley fold and unfold.

5 Rabbit ear fold.

6 Mountain fold.

7 Valley fold into the top pockets.

8 Mountain fold.

9 Valley fold and unfold. There are no guide folds for this step.

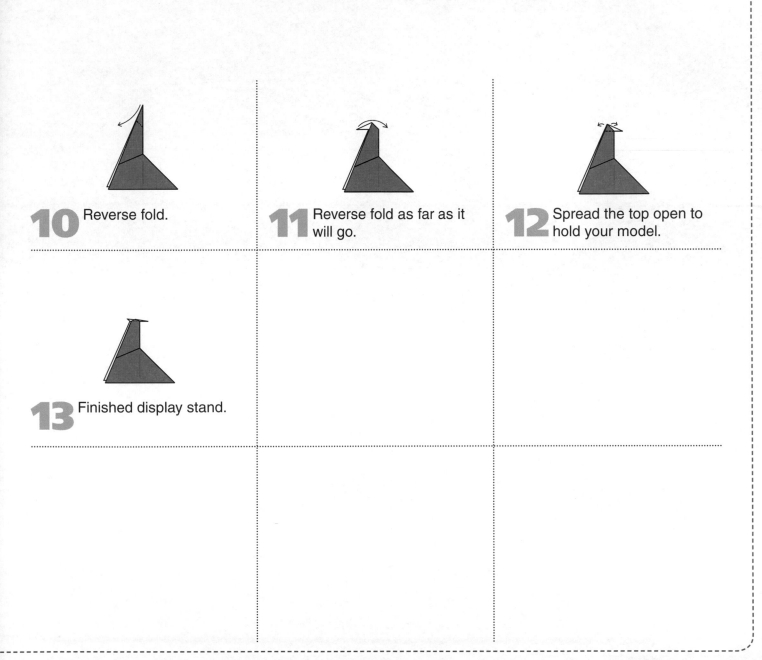

10 Reverse fold.

11 Reverse fold as far as it will go.

12 Spread the top open to hold your model.

13 Finished display stand.

PART TWO

THE PROJECTS

"You know, sometimes I amaze even myself."
—HAN SOLO

HAN SOLO

A smuggler, a scoundrel, and a hero of the Rebel Alliance—Han Solo played all of these roles with equal enthusiasm. As a young man, Han was kicked out of the Imperial Academy for defying orders to kill the Wookiee Chewbacca, an act that sparked a life-long friendship. Han first met Luke Skywalker when Luke needed to hire a good pilot and a fast ship. This was how Han found himself in the middle of the Rebellion that he had no interest in, and in the end turned out to be quite heroic. Not only did he help rescue Princess Leia Organa, he was also instrumental in the destruction of both Death Stars and the eventual collapse of the Empire—even if he did spend some time on Jabba the Hutt's wall, encased in a carbonite block.

HOW TO FOLD: HAN SOLO

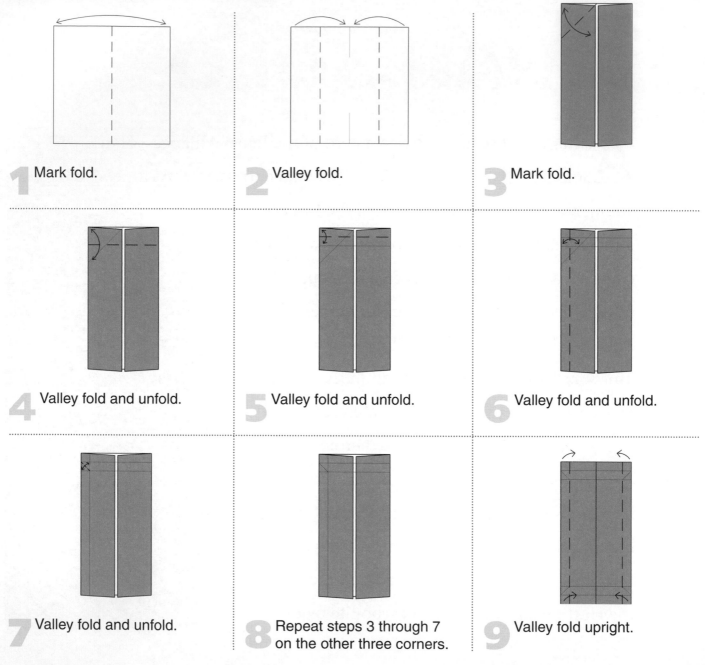

1 Mark fold.

2 Valley fold.

3 Mark fold.

4 Valley fold and unfold.

5 Valley fold and unfold.

6 Valley fold and unfold.

7 Valley fold and unfold.

8 Repeat steps 3 through 7 on the other three corners.

9 Valley fold upright.

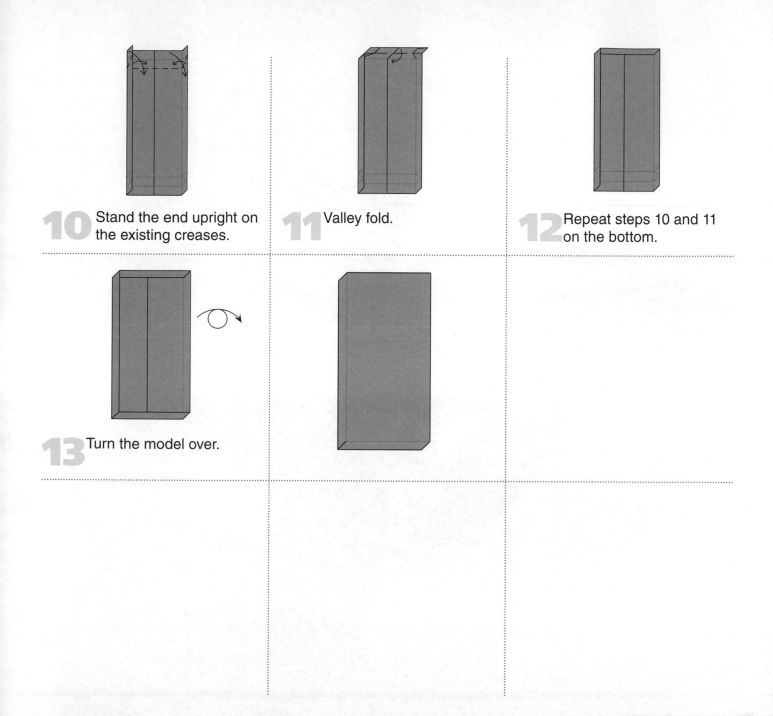

10 Stand the end upright on the existing creases.

11 Valley fold.

12 Repeat steps 10 and 11 on the bottom.

13 Turn the model over.

"No disintegrations."
—DARTH VADER TO BOBA FETT

JANGO FETT AND BOBA FETT

Jango Fett was a Mandalorian warrior who became a legendary bounty hunter. Ruthless yet honorable, he was selected by Darth Tyranus (Count Dooku) to become the genetic template for the clone army of the Republic. Aside from a cash payment, Jango also asked for an unaltered clone that he could raise as his son. Following in his father's footsteps, Boba Fett became the most notorious bounty hunter in the galaxy. While his armor looked battered and worn, it held many hidden weapons, including rocket darts, a flamethrower, and a rocket pack with a guided missile. But the most effective weapon the Fetts used was their cunning, preferring to outwit and trap their quarry rather than use pure force.

Boba Fett

Jango Fett

HOW TO FOLD: JANGO FETT AND BOBA FETT

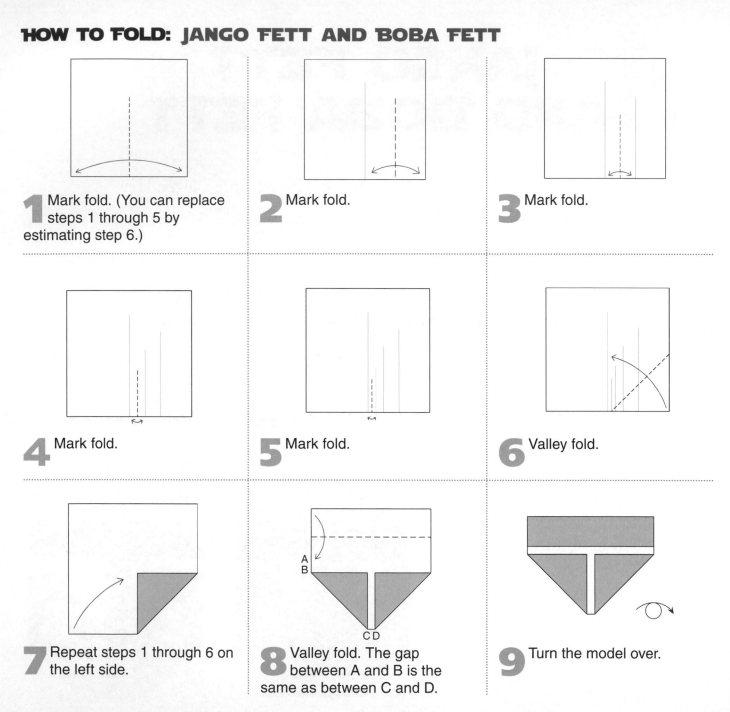

1 Mark fold. (You can replace steps 1 through 5 by estimating step 6.)

2 Mark fold.

3 Mark fold.

4 Mark fold.

5 Mark fold.

6 Valley fold.

7 Repeat steps 1 through 6 on the left side.

8 Valley fold. The gap between A and B is the same as between C and D.

9 Turn the model over.

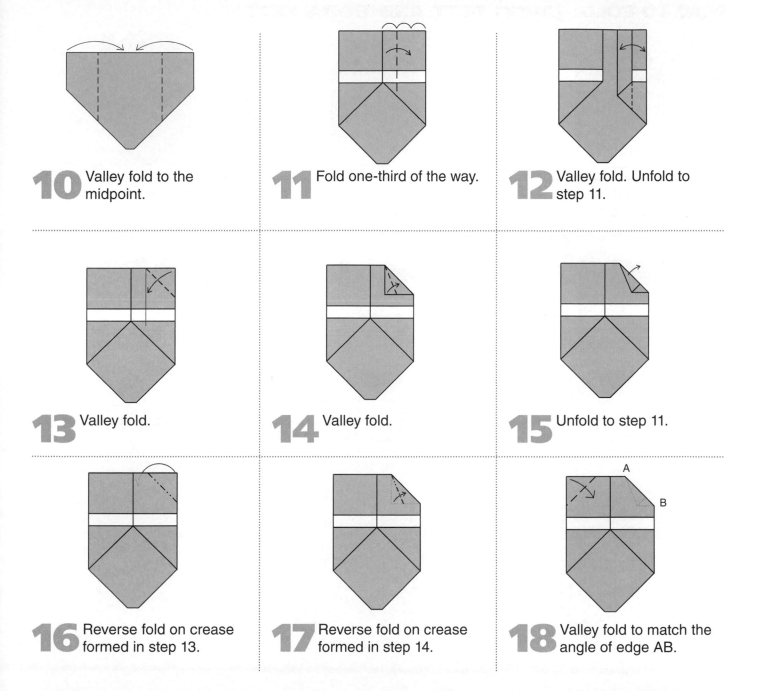

10 Valley fold to the midpoint.

11 Fold one-third of the way.

12 Valley fold. Unfold to step 11.

13 Valley fold.

14 Valley fold.

15 Unfold to step 11.

16 Reverse fold on crease formed in step 13.

17 Reverse fold on crease formed in step 14.

18 Valley fold to match the angle of edge AB.

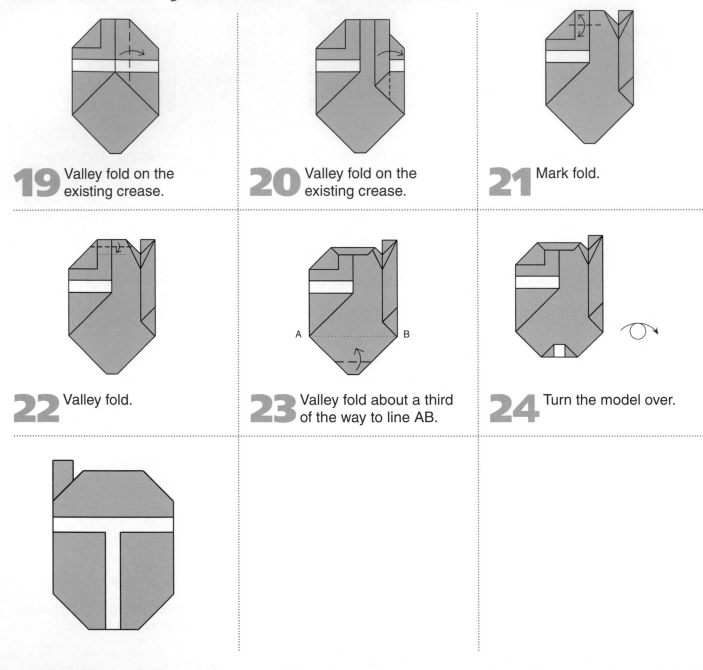

19 Valley fold on the existing crease.

20 Valley fold on the existing crease.

21 Mark fold.

22 Valley fold.

23 Valley fold about a third of the way to line AB.

24 Turn the model over.

TEST YOUR STAR WARS IQ:
MATCHUP

Match the *Star Wars* character to his or her home planet.

1. Padmé Amidala   **A.** Tatooine

2. Chewbacca   **B.** Stewjon

3. Luke Skywalker   **C.** Alderaan

4. Boba Fett   **D.** Kamino

5. Obi-Wan Kenobi   **E.** Naboo

6. Princess Leia Organa   **F.** Corellia

7. Han Solo   **G.** Kashyyyk

"[The Force's] energy surrounds us and binds us. Luminous beings are we, not this crude matter."

—YODA

YODA

A Master of the Jedi Council, Yoda was inarguably one of the most powerful Jedi of all time. For more than eight hundred years he trained Jedi Knights, until the Republic collapsed. When the new Emperor Palpatine instituted Order 66, calling for the execution of all the Jedi, only Yoda and Obi-Wan Kenobi managed to survive. After Yoda failed to defeat Palpatine, he exiled himself on the swamp planet, Dagobah, hiding until the time was right to restore the Jedi Order. This was where he met and trained Luke Skywalker in the ways of the Force. Yoda was the last of the original Jedi, and Luke was his last Padawan.

HOW TO FOLD: YODA

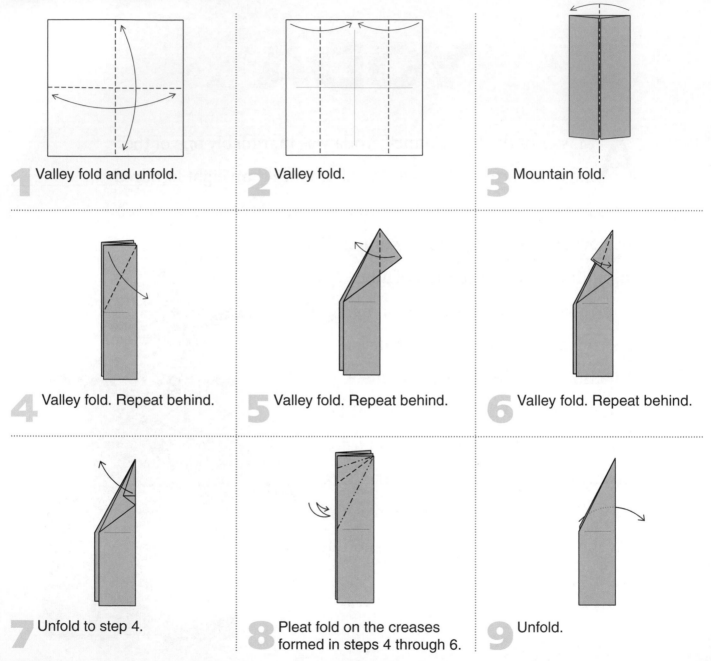

1 Valley fold and unfold.

2 Valley fold.

3 Mountain fold.

4 Valley fold. Repeat behind.

5 Valley fold. Repeat behind.

6 Valley fold. Repeat behind.

7 Unfold to step 4.

8 Pleat fold on the creases formed in steps 4 through 6.

9 Unfold.

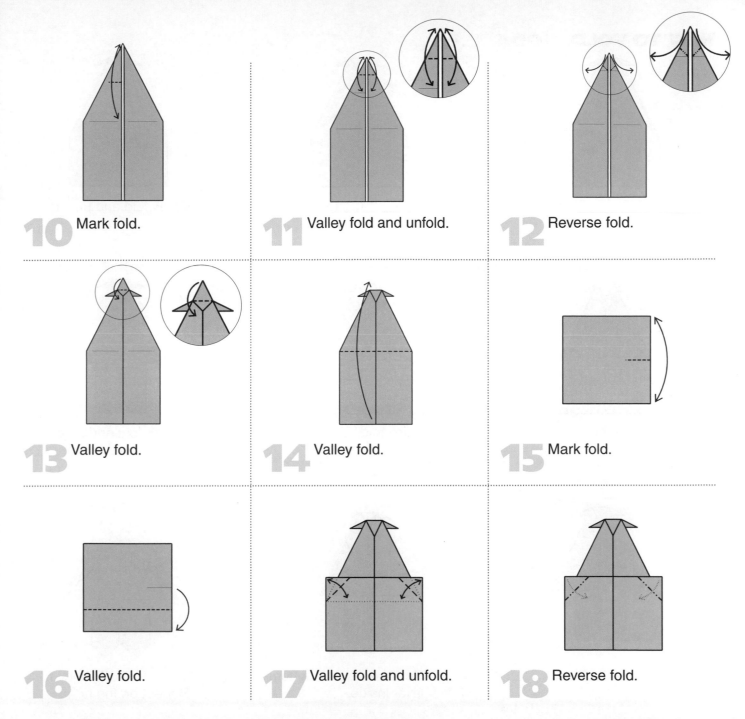

10 Mark fold.

11 Valley fold and unfold.

12 Reverse fold.

13 Valley fold.

14 Valley fold.

15 Mark fold.

16 Valley fold.

17 Valley fold and unfold.

18 Reverse fold.

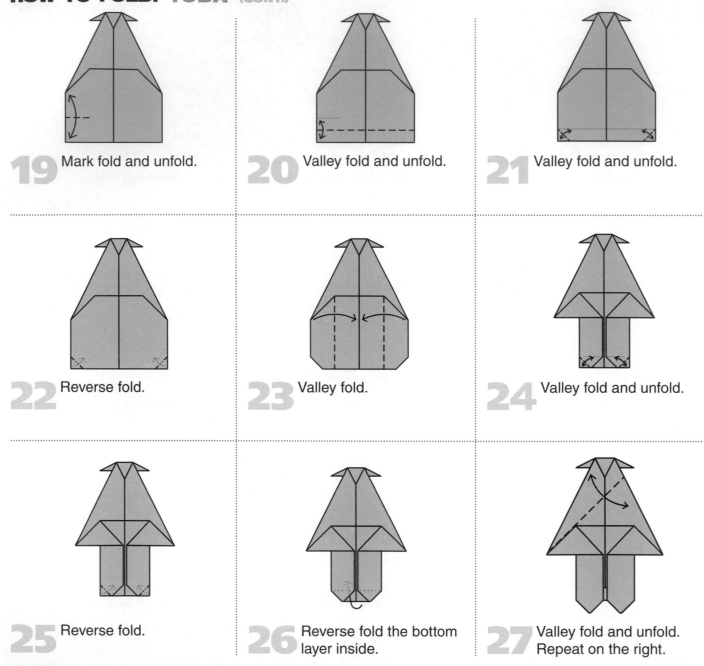

19 Mark fold and unfold.

20 Valley fold and unfold.

21 Valley fold and unfold.

22 Reverse fold.

23 Valley fold.

24 Valley fold and unfold.

25 Reverse fold.

26 Reverse fold the bottom layer inside.

27 Valley fold and unfold. Repeat on the right.

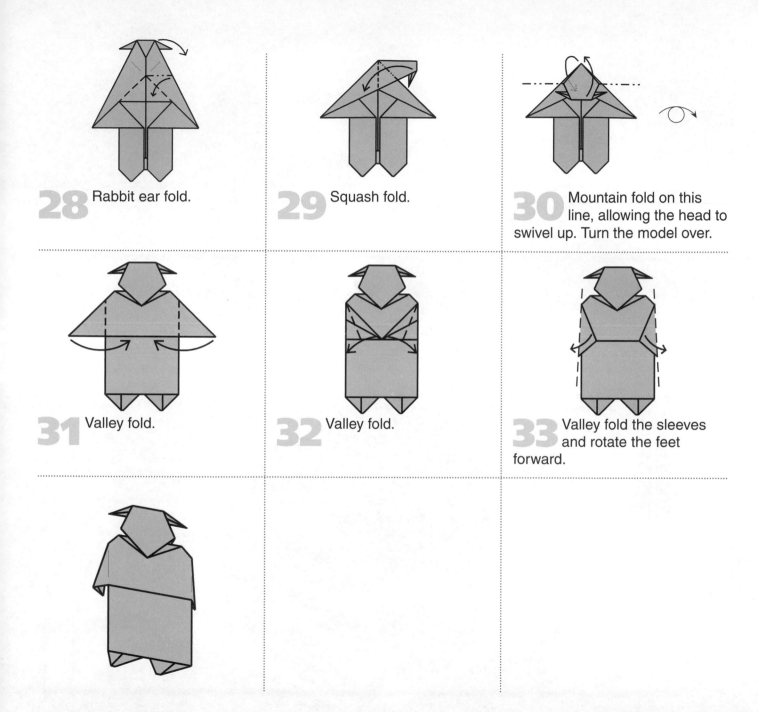

28 Rabbit ear fold.

29 Squash fold.

30 Mountain fold on this line, allowing the head to swivel up. Turn the model over.

31 Valley fold.

32 Valley fold.

33 Valley fold the sleeves and rotate the feet forward.

"I do believe they think I am some sort of god."

—C-3PO

C-3PO

Like all protocol droids, C-3PO specialized in interpretation and communication with intelligent species and droids throughout the galaxy. Fluent in more than six million galactic languages, he was most drawn to the nuances of human interaction. And while C-3PO might have been a bit fussy, he was incredibly loyal to his masters and his counterpart, R2-D2. Originally built from parts that a young Anakin Skywalker scavenged in Watto's junkyard, C-3PO stayed in the extended Skywalker family, working for Padmé Amidala, Bail Organa, Princess Leia Organa, and Luke Skywalker.

NOTE: You will need two pieces of paper for this model. Steps 1 through 19 form the lower half. Steps 20 through 51 form the upper half.

HOW TO FOLD: C-3PO

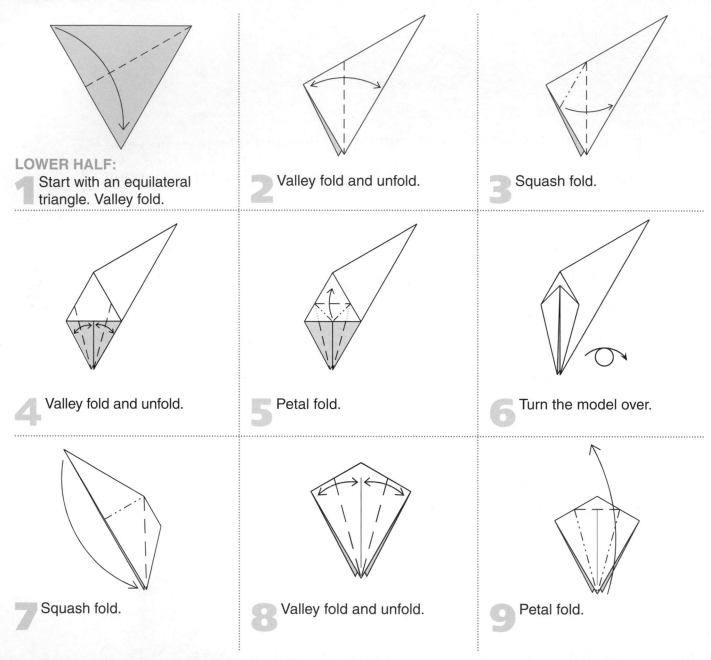

LOWER HALF:

1 Start with an equilateral triangle. Valley fold.

2 Valley fold and unfold.

3 Squash fold.

4 Valley fold and unfold.

5 Petal fold.

6 Turn the model over.

7 Squash fold.

8 Valley fold and unfold.

9 Petal fold.

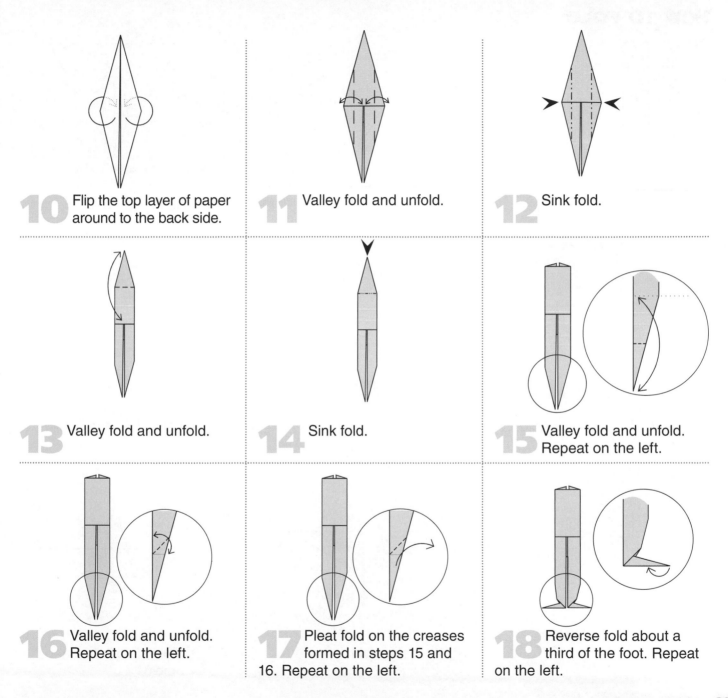

10 Flip the top layer of paper around to the back side.

11 Valley fold and unfold.

12 Sink fold.

13 Valley fold and unfold.

14 Sink fold.

15 Valley fold and unfold. Repeat on the left.

16 Valley fold and unfold. Repeat on the left.

17 Pleat fold on the creases formed in steps 15 and 16. Repeat on the left.

18 Reverse fold about a third of the foot. Repeat on the left.

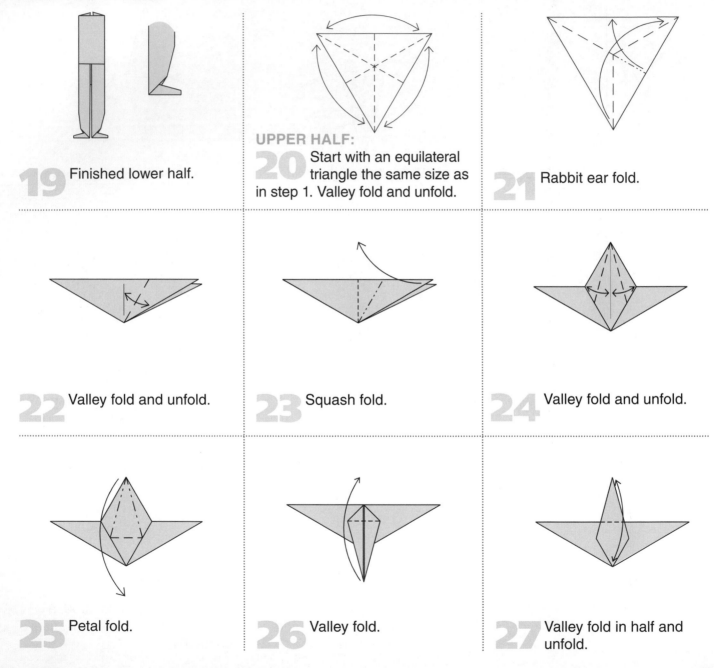

19 Finished lower half.

UPPER HALF:

20 Start with an equilateral triangle the same size as in step 1. Valley fold and unfold.

21 Rabbit ear fold.

22 Valley fold and unfold.

23 Squash fold.

24 Valley fold and unfold.

25 Petal fold.

26 Valley fold.

27 Valley fold in half and unfold.

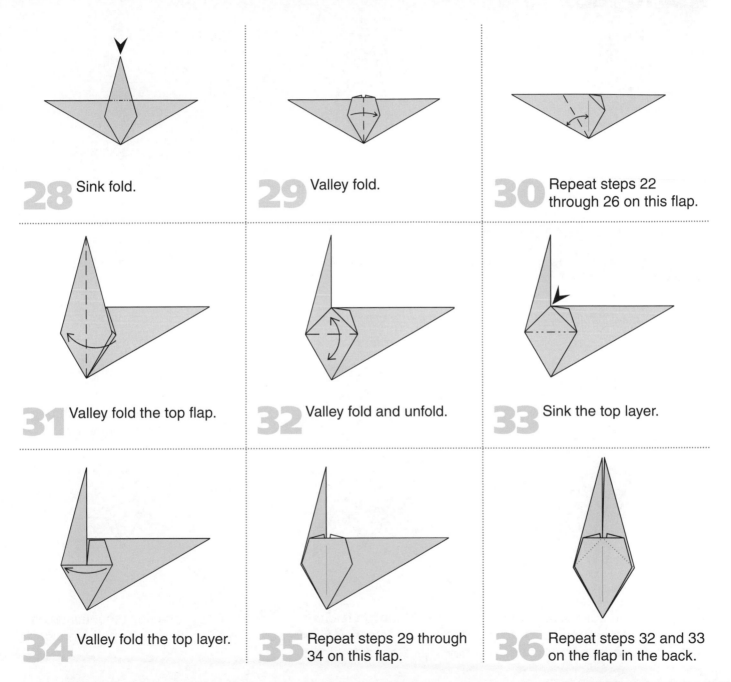

28 Sink fold.

29 Valley fold.

30 Repeat steps 22 through 26 on this flap.

31 Valley fold the top flap.

32 Valley fold and unfold.

33 Sink the top layer.

34 Valley fold the top layer.

35 Repeat steps 29 through 34 on this flap.

36 Repeat steps 32 and 33 on the flap in the back.

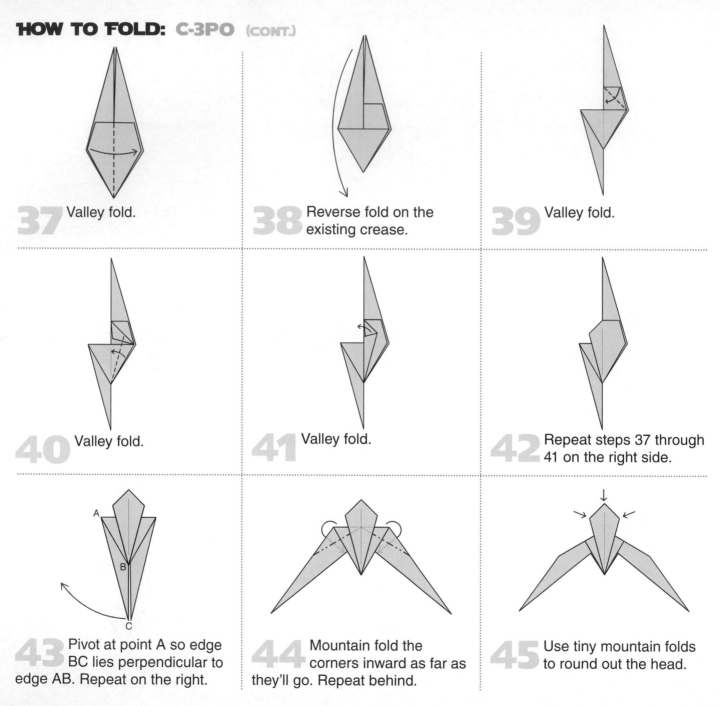

37 Valley fold.

38 Reverse fold on the existing crease.

39 Valley fold.

40 Valley fold.

41 Valley fold.

42 Repeat steps 37 through 41 on the right side.

43 Pivot at point A so edge BC lies perpendicular to edge AB. Repeat on the right.

44 Mountain fold the corners inward as far as they'll go. Repeat behind.

45 Use tiny mountain folds to round out the head.

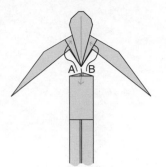

46 Insert the upper half into the pocket of the lower half, while inserting tabs A and B into the top pockets of the lower half. Keep the tabs above the arms.

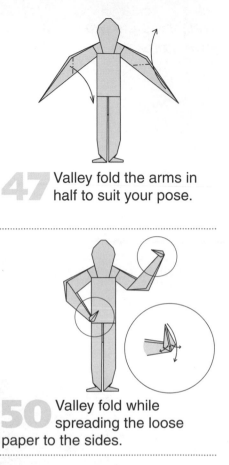

47 Valley fold the arms in half to suit your pose.

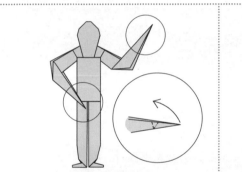

48 Squash fold about one-fourth of the arm to form hands.

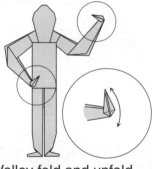

49 Valley fold and unfold.

50 Valley fold while spreading the loose paper to the sides.

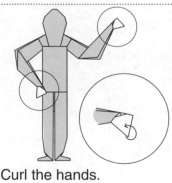

51 Curl the hands.

"Well, there are two banthas
down there. . . . "
—LUKE SKYWALKER

BANTHA

Banthas were giant beasts that roamed the deserts of Tatooine in herds of fifteen or more. Their thick fur coats, long tails, and curved horns enabled them to survive Tatooine's hostile climate and vicious predators. The Sand People, or Tusken Raiders, domesticated the bantha and used them primarily for transportation. On raiding parties, the Sand People rode them single file to hide their numbers.

HOW TO FOLD: BANTHA

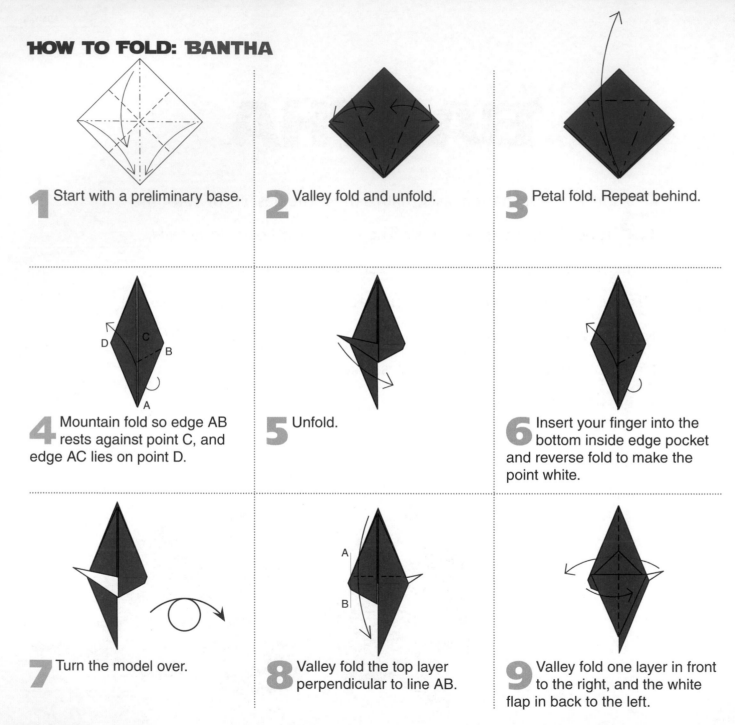

1 Start with a preliminary base.

2 Valley fold and unfold.

3 Petal fold. Repeat behind.

4 Mountain fold so edge AB rests against point C, and edge AC lies on point D.

5 Unfold.

6 Insert your finger into the bottom inside edge pocket and reverse fold to make the point white.

7 Turn the model over.

8 Valley fold the top layer perpendicular to line AB.

9 Valley fold one layer in front to the right, and the white flap in back to the left.

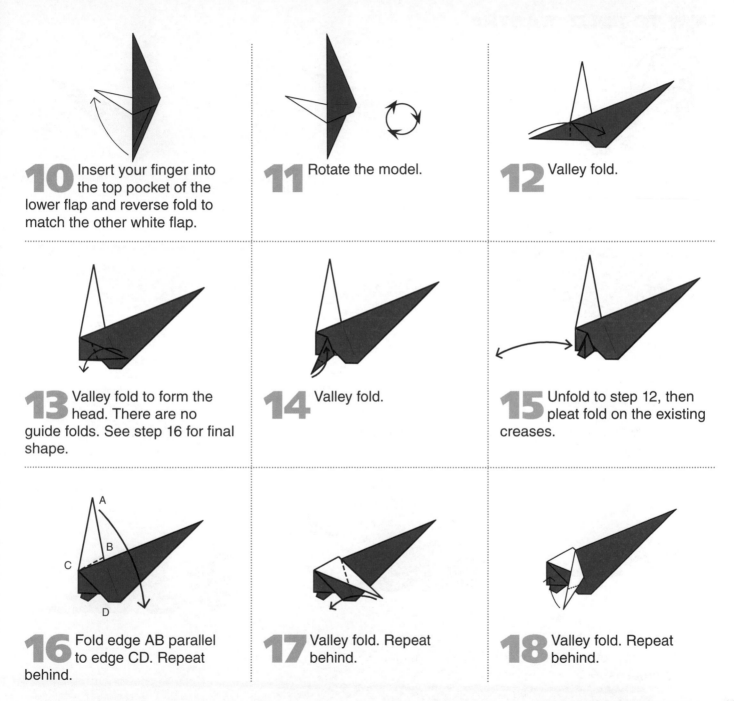

10 Insert your finger into the top pocket of the lower flap and reverse fold to match the other white flap.

11 Rotate the model.

12 Valley fold.

13 Valley fold to form the head. There are no guide folds. See step 16 for final shape.

14 Valley fold.

15 Unfold to step 12, then pleat fold on the existing creases.

16 Fold edge AB parallel to edge CD. Repeat behind.

17 Valley fold. Repeat behind.

18 Valley fold. Repeat behind.

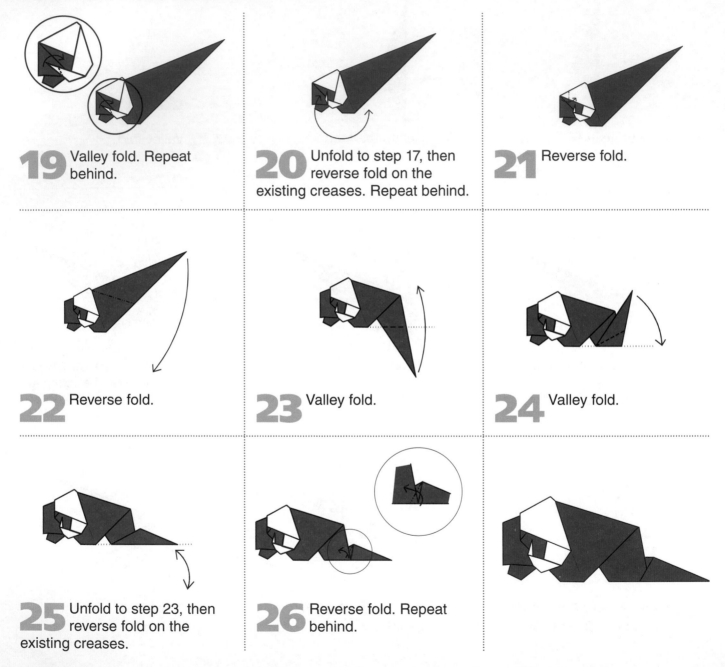

19 Valley fold. Repeat behind.

20 Unfold to step 17, then reverse fold on the existing creases. Repeat behind.

21 Reverse fold.

22 Reverse fold.

23 Valley fold.

24 Valley fold.

25 Unfold to step 23, then reverse fold on the existing creases.

26 Reverse fold. Repeat behind.

TEST YOUR STAR WARS IQ:
MATCHUP

Match the *Star Wars* character to his or her weapon of choice.

1. Anakin Skywalker **A.** Red-bladed lightsaber

2. Darth Vader **B.** Sporting blaster

3. Princess Leia Organa **C.** Blue-bladed lightsaber

4. Mace Windu **D.** DL-44 heavy blaster pistol

5. Han Solo **E.** Purple-bladed lightsaber

6. Yoda **F.** EE-3 blaster rifle

7. Boba Fett **G.** Green-bladed lightsaber

ANSWERS: 1.C, 2.A, 3.B, 4.E, 5.D, 6.G, 7.F

"I'd just as soon kiss a Wookiee."
—PRINCESS LEIA ORGANA

PRINCESS LEIA ORGANA

Princess Leia Organa was adopted at birth by Senator Bail Organa and Queen Breha, Alderaan's ruling family. Beautiful, smart, and outspoken, Leia became a key figure in intergalactic politics and in the rebellion against the Empire. On one such mission, Leia was captured by Darth Vader. In spite of being tortured and forced to watch the complete destruction of Alderaan, she never revealed the rebellion's secrets and was sentenced to death. While awaiting execution, she was rescued by Luke Skywalker and Han Solo. Leia was later shocked to discover that Darth Vader was her real father, Luke Skywalker was her twin brother, and that she had the potential to become one of the legendary Jedi Knights.

HOW TO FOLD: PRINCESS LEIA ORGANA

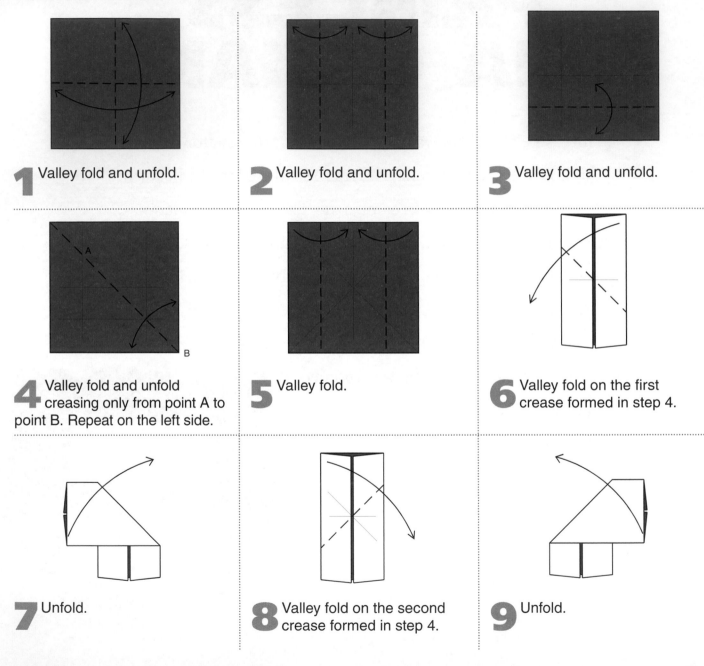

1 Valley fold and unfold.

2 Valley fold and unfold.

3 Valley fold and unfold.

4 Valley fold and unfold creasing only from point A to point B. Repeat on the left side.

5 Valley fold.

6 Valley fold on the first crease formed in step 4.

7 Unfold.

8 Valley fold on the second crease formed in step 4.

9 Unfold.

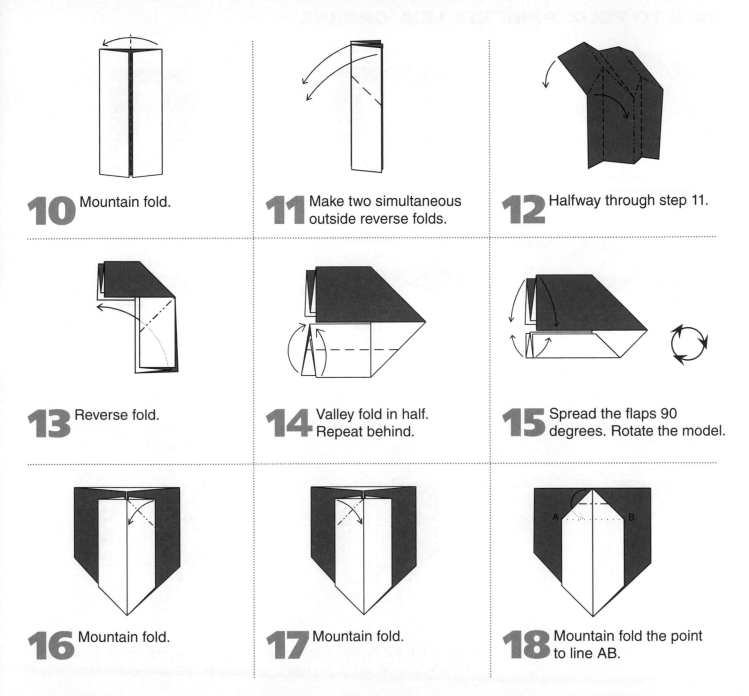

10 Mountain fold.

11 Make two simultaneous outside reverse folds.

12 Halfway through step 11.

13 Reverse fold.

14 Valley fold in half. Repeat behind.

15 Spread the flaps 90 degrees. Rotate the model.

16 Mountain fold.

17 Mountain fold.

18 Mountain fold the point to line AB.

HOW TO FOLD: PRINCESS LEIA ORGANA (CONT.)

19 Mountain fold.

20 Valley fold.

21 Valley fold about one-fifth of the way.

22 Valley fold and unfold.

23 Reverse fold.

24 Mountain fold the corner.

25 Round out the corner with a mountain fold.

26 Lift the hidden part of the face on top of the hair.

27 Repeat steps 20 through 26 on the left side.

Princess Leia being held captive by Darth Vader.

"I don't know—fly casual."
—HAN SOLO TO CHEWBACCA

CHEWBACCA

A Wookiee from the planet Kashyyyk, Chewbacca was a hero of the Rebellion from the earliest days. Assigned to Yoda as a bodyguard during the Clone Wars, Chewbacca helped him escape when Chancellor Palpatine called for the death of all Jedi. While on the run from the Imperial forces, Chewbacca was captured by Trandoshan slavers. During this time, Chewbacca met Han Solo, who freed him and saved his life. Chewbacca swore a life-debt to Han and became Han's copilot, and the two grew to be friends. Later, Chewbacca was once again drawn into the Rebellion when he and Han met Luke Skywalker, helped rescue Princess Leia Organa, and together destroyed the Death Star.

NOTE: You need two pieces of paper for this model. Steps 1 through 19 form the lower half. Steps 20 through 51 form the upper half.

HOW TO FOLD: CHEWBACCA

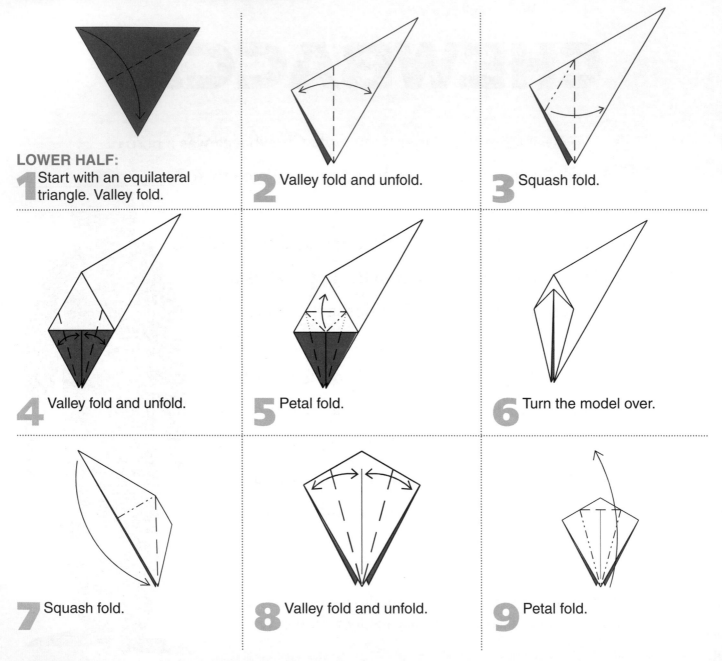

LOWER HALF:

1 Start with an equilateral triangle. Valley fold.

2 Valley fold and unfold.

3 Squash fold.

4 Valley fold and unfold.

5 Petal fold.

6 Turn the model over.

7 Squash fold.

8 Valley fold and unfold.

9 Petal fold.

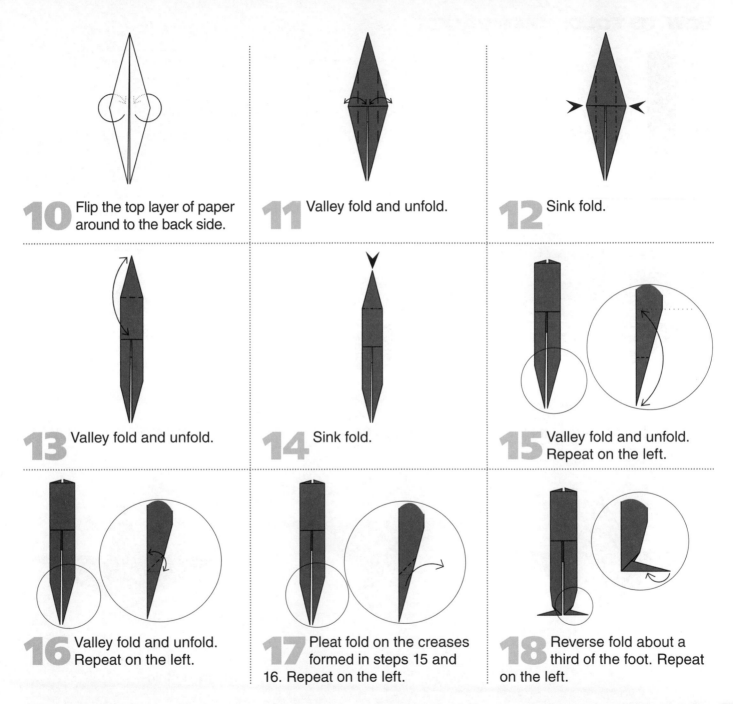

10 Flip the top layer of paper around to the back side.

11 Valley fold and unfold.

12 Sink fold.

13 Valley fold and unfold.

14 Sink fold.

15 Valley fold and unfold. Repeat on the left.

16 Valley fold and unfold. Repeat on the left.

17 Pleat fold on the creases formed in steps 15 and 16. Repeat on the left.

18 Reverse fold about a third of the foot. Repeat on the left.

HOW TO FOLD: CHEWBACCA (CONT.)

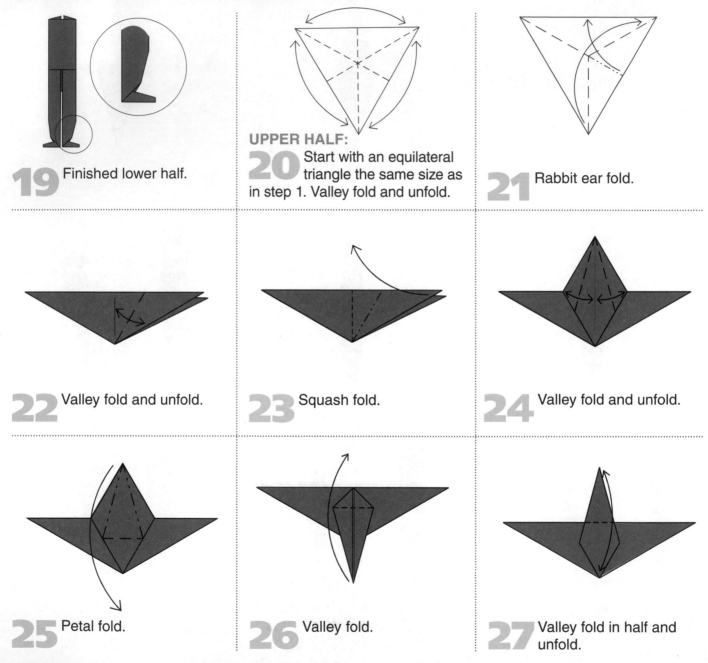

19 Finished lower half.

UPPER HALF:
20 Start with an equilateral triangle the same size as in step 1. Valley fold and unfold.

21 Rabbit ear fold.

22 Valley fold and unfold.

23 Squash fold.

24 Valley fold and unfold.

25 Petal fold.

26 Valley fold.

27 Valley fold in half and unfold.

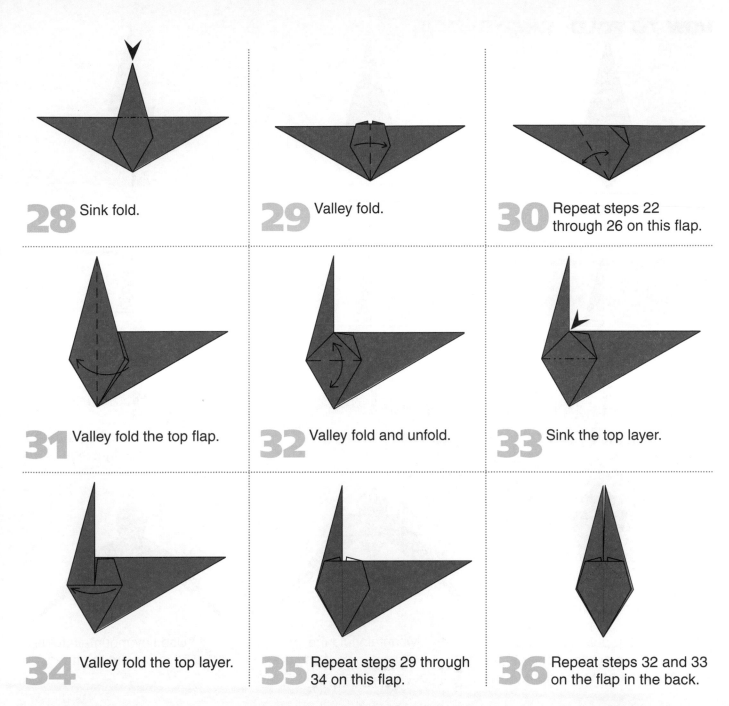

28 Sink fold.

29 Valley fold.

30 Repeat steps 22 through 26 on this flap.

31 Valley fold the top flap.

32 Valley fold and unfold.

33 Sink the top layer.

34 Valley fold the top layer.

35 Repeat steps 29 through 34 on this flap.

36 Repeat steps 32 and 33 on the flap in the back.

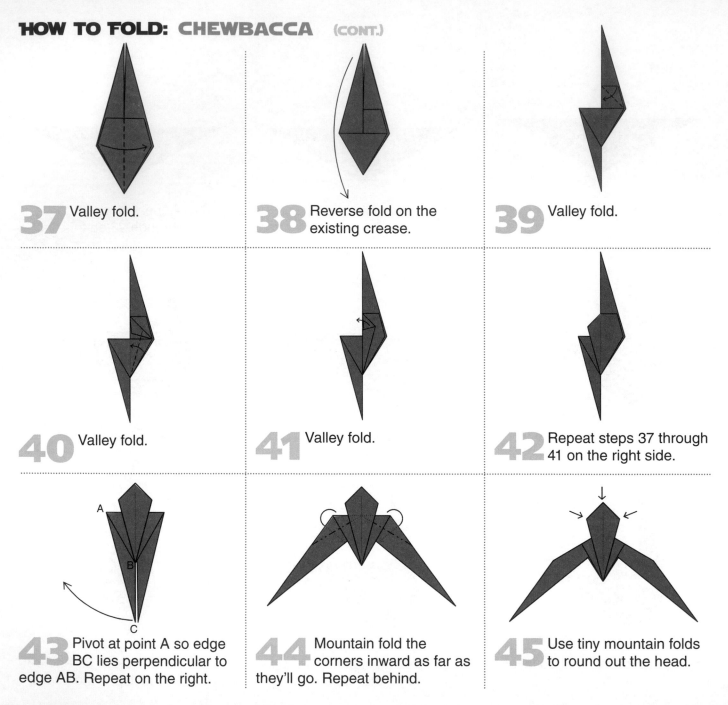

37 Valley fold.

38 Reverse fold on the existing crease.

39 Valley fold.

40 Valley fold.

41 Valley fold.

42 Repeat steps 37 through 41 on the right side.

43 Pivot at point A so edge BC lies perpendicular to edge AB. Repeat on the right.

44 Mountain fold the corners inward as far as they'll go. Repeat behind.

45 Use tiny mountain folds to round out the head.

46 Insert the upper half into the pocket of the lower half, while inserting tabs A and B into the top pockets of the lower half. Keep the tabs above the arms.

47 Valley fold the arms in half to suit your pose.

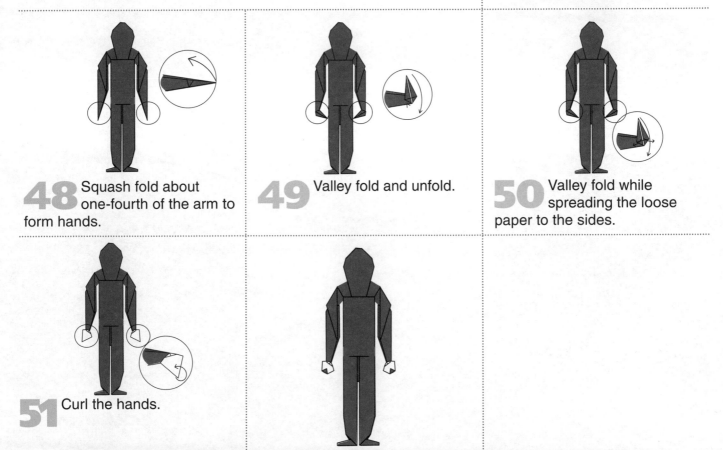

48 Squash fold about one-fourth of the arm to form hands.

49 Valley fold and unfold.

50 Valley fold while spreading the loose paper to the sides.

51 Curl the hands.

"The dark side of the Force is a pathway to many abilities some consider to be unnatural."

—PALPATINE

DARTH SIDIOUS (EMPEROR PALPATINE)

Palpatine began his rise to power as the Senator of Naboo, eventually becoming Supreme Chancellor of the Galactic Republic. Then with his Sith apprentice, Darth Tyranus, he orchestrated a civil war. Half of the planetary systems remained loyal to him and the Republic, the other half followed Tyranus and the Separatists. With the galaxy in turmoil, the Jedi were spread thin leading the clone army against the Separatists. Sidious then seduced a confused Anakin Skywalker over to the dark side of the Force. With Anakin's help, the Jedi were destroyed, and Sidious announced the war was over. He brought an end to the Galactic Republic, declared himself Emperor Palpatine, and plunged the galaxy into darkness.

HOW TO FOLD: DARTH SIDIOUS (EMPEROR PALPATINE)

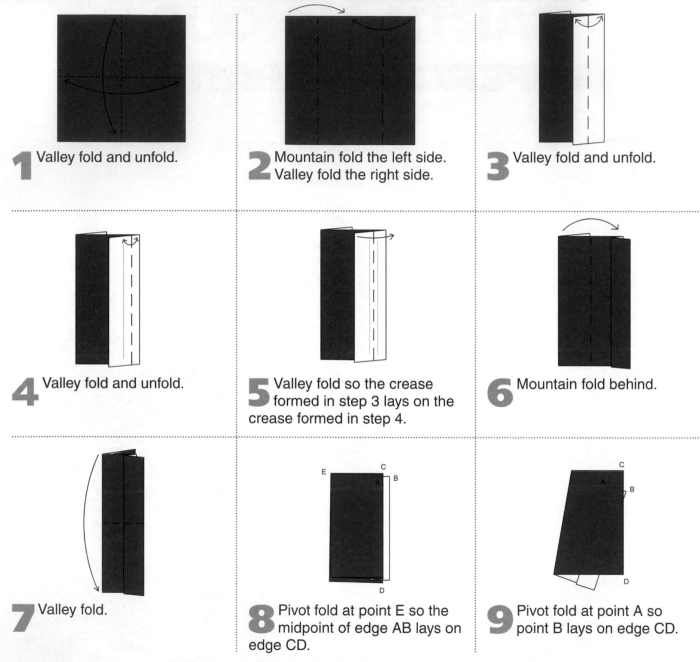

1 Valley fold and unfold.

2 Mountain fold the left side. Valley fold the right side.

3 Valley fold and unfold.

4 Valley fold and unfold.

5 Valley fold so the crease formed in step 3 lays on the crease formed in step 4.

6 Mountain fold behind.

7 Valley fold.

8 Pivot fold at point E so the midpoint of edge AB lays on edge CD.

9 Pivot fold at point A so point B lays on edge CD.

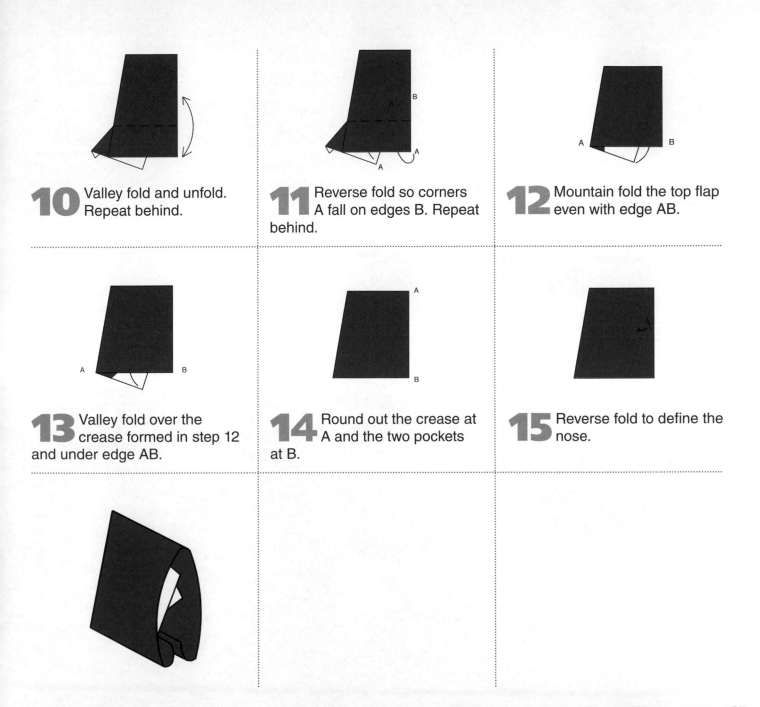

10 Valley fold and unfold. Repeat behind.

11 Reverse fold so corners A fall on edges B. Repeat behind.

12 Mountain fold the top flap even with edge AB.

13 Valley fold over the crease formed in step 12 and under edge AB.

14 Round out the crease at A and the two pockets at B.

15 Reverse fold to define the nose.

"An extremely well-put-together little droid, Your Highness."

—CAPTAIN PANA
TO QUEEN AMIDA

R2-D2

R2-D2, a bold, loyal, and spirited astromech droid, understood most forms of speech—but he spoke in a series of electronic chirps, whistles, and squeaks. And though astromechs were typically designed for starship management and repair, R2-D2's loyalty to Padmé and her family, and his long friendship with C-3PO, made him unique. That, and R2-D2 always seemed to be at the center of events in the galaxy. He repaired the shields on Queen Amidala's starship, allowing her to escape from Naboo. He carried the Death Star plans to the rebels and was on Luke's X-wing when Luke destroyed the Death Star. This little droid saved the lives of Padmé, Anakin, Luke, Han, and Leia.

HOW TO FOLD: R2-D2

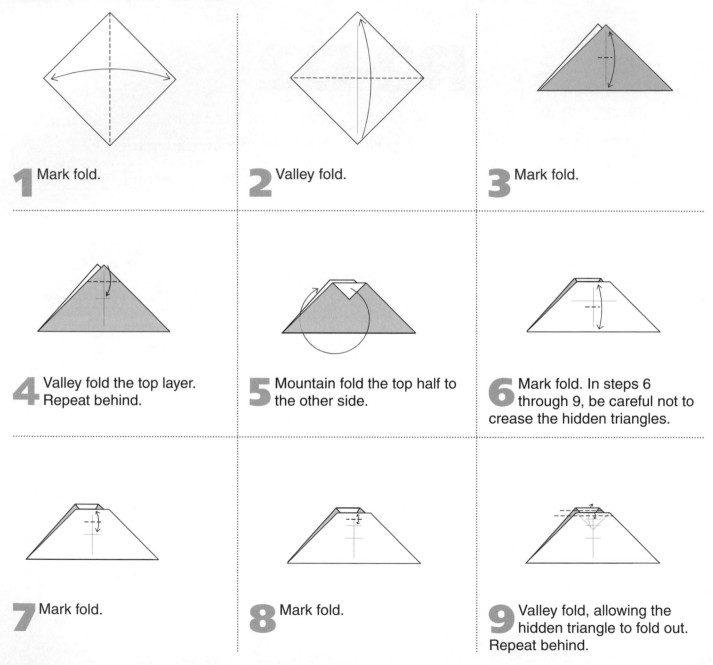

1 Mark fold.

2 Valley fold.

3 Mark fold.

4 Valley fold the top layer. Repeat behind.

5 Mountain fold the top half to the other side.

6 Mark fold. In steps 6 through 9, be careful not to crease the hidden triangles.

7 Mark fold.

8 Mark fold.

9 Valley fold, allowing the hidden triangle to fold out. Repeat behind.

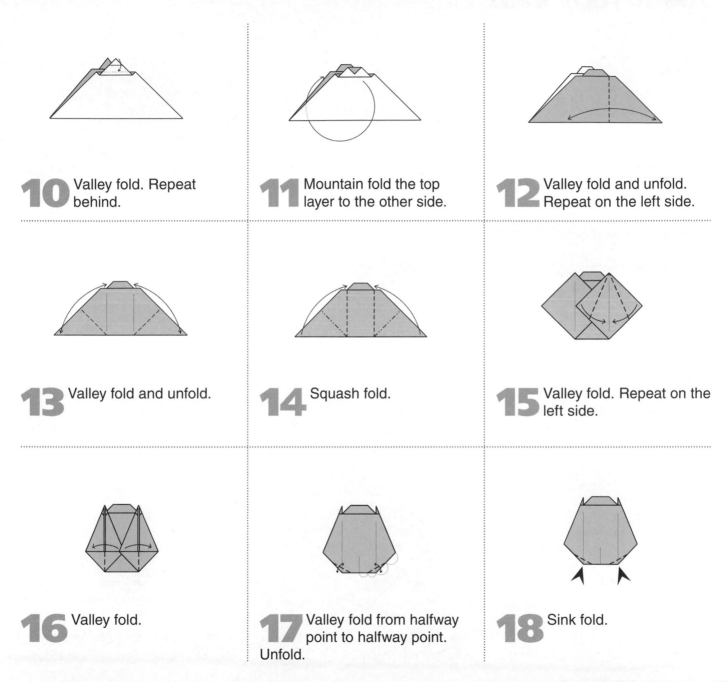

10 Valley fold. Repeat behind.

11 Mountain fold the top layer to the other side.

12 Valley fold and unfold. Repeat on the left side.

13 Valley fold and unfold.

14 Squash fold.

15 Valley fold. Repeat on the left side.

16 Valley fold.

17 Valley fold from halfway point to halfway point. Unfold.

18 Sink fold.

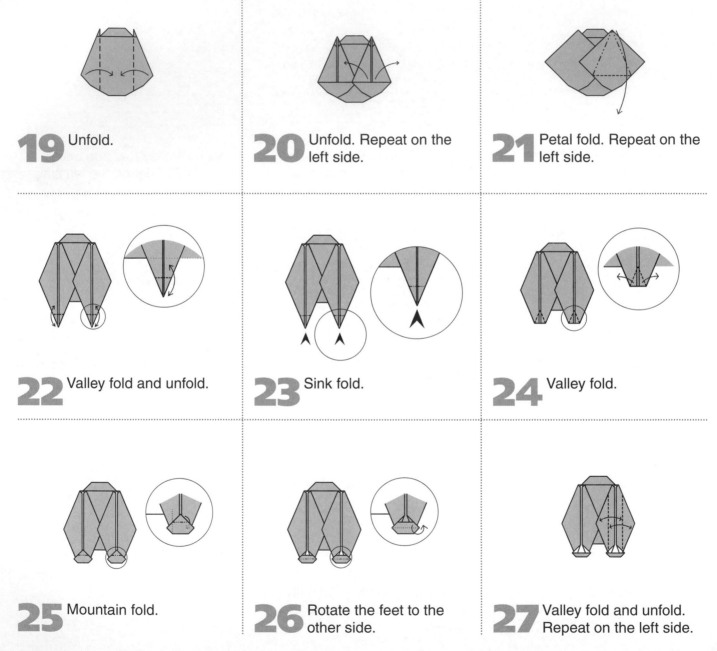

19 Unfold.

20 Unfold. Repeat on the left side.

21 Petal fold. Repeat on the left side.

22 Valley fold and unfold.

23 Sink fold.

24 Valley fold.

25 Mountain fold.

26 Rotate the feet to the other side.

27 Valley fold and unfold. Repeat on the left side.

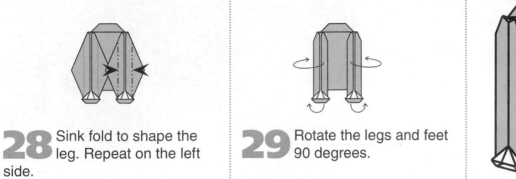

28 Sink fold to shape the leg. Repeat on the left side.

29 Rotate the legs and feet 90 degrees.

R2-D2 repairing the shields on Queen Amidala's starship.

"I shall enjoy watching you die."
—JABBA THE HUTT TO
LUKE SKYWALKER

JABBA THE HUTT

atooine's most infamous resident was Jabba the Hutt. The sluglike crime lord controlled a vast array of illegal activities, including slavery, extortion, gambling, and, of course, spice-running. Han Solo used to be one of Jabba's smugglers until, on a run, Han was about to be boarded by the authorities and was forced to jettison the spice he was carrying. Jabba demanded he pay for the lost shipment, and when Han couldn't, Jabba placed a bounty on his head. The bounty hunter Boba Fett presented Han encased in a carbonite block to Jabba, which he very happily displayed on his palace wall.

HOW TO FOLD: JABBA THE HUTT

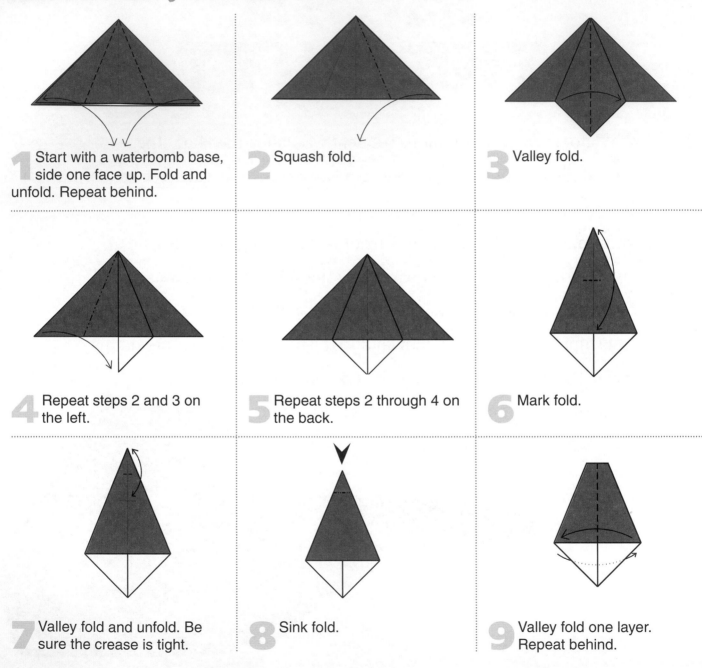

1 Start with a waterbomb base, side one face up. Fold and unfold. Repeat behind.

2 Squash fold.

3 Valley fold.

4 Repeat steps 2 and 3 on the left.

5 Repeat steps 2 through 4 on the back.

6 Mark fold.

7 Valley fold and unfold. Be sure the crease is tight.

8 Sink fold.

9 Valley fold one layer. Repeat behind.

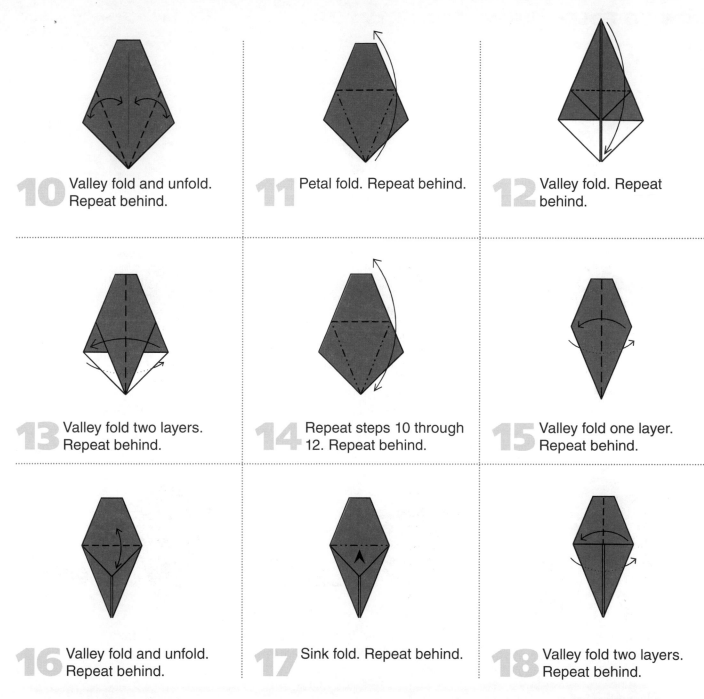

10 Valley fold and unfold. Repeat behind.

11 Petal fold. Repeat behind.

12 Valley fold. Repeat behind.

13 Valley fold two layers. Repeat behind.

14 Repeat steps 10 through 12. Repeat behind.

15 Valley fold one layer. Repeat behind.

16 Valley fold and unfold. Repeat behind.

17 Sink fold. Repeat behind.

18 Valley fold two layers. Repeat behind.

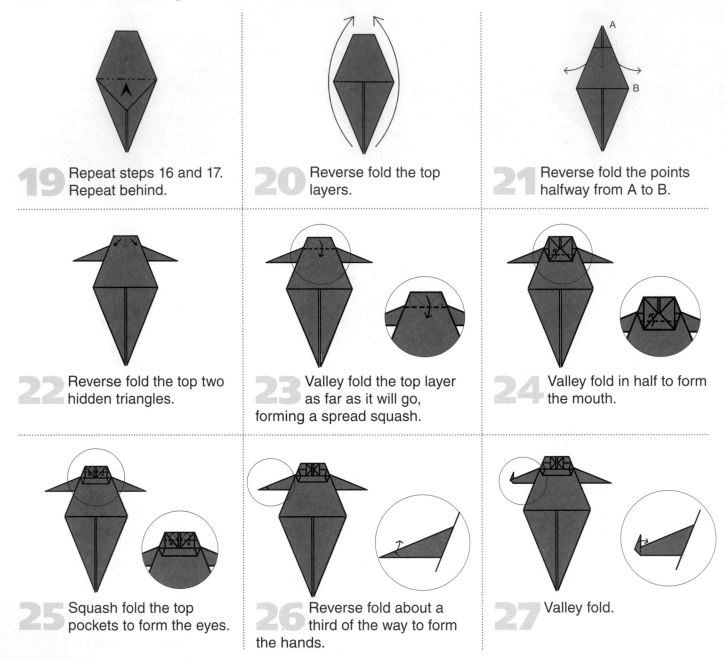

19 Repeat steps 16 and 17. Repeat behind.

20 Reverse fold the top layers.

21 Reverse fold the points halfway from A to B.

22 Reverse fold the top two hidden triangles.

23 Valley fold the top layer as far as it will go, forming a spread squash.

24 Valley fold in half to form the mouth.

25 Squash fold the top pockets to form the eyes.

26 Reverse fold about a third of the way to form the hands.

27 Valley fold.

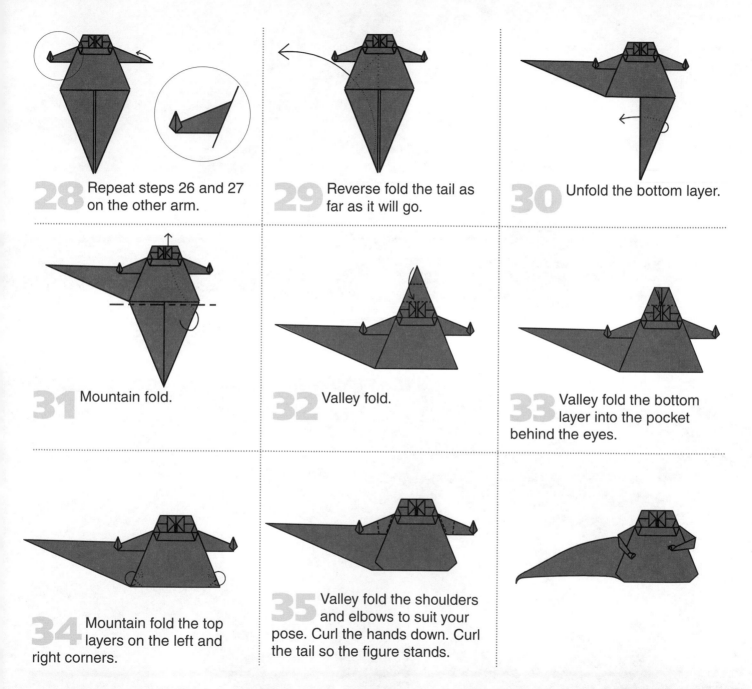

28 Repeat steps 26 and 27 on the other arm.

29 Reverse fold the tail as far as it will go.

30 Unfold the bottom layer.

31 Mountain fold.

32 Valley fold.

33 Valley fold the bottom layer into the pocket behind the eyes.

34 Mountain fold the top layers on the left and right corners.

35 Valley fold the shoulders and elbows to suit your pose. Curl the hands down. Curl the tail so the figure stands.

"If you only knew the power of the dark side."

—DARTH VADER

DARTH VADER

Darth Vader, Dark Lord of the Sith, wasn't always evil. Born Anakin Skywalker, he was once a pupil of Obi-Wan Kenobi— the Chosen One spoken of in an ancient Jedi prophecy. But when Supreme Chancellor Palpatine (Darth Sidious) convinced Anakin that the only way to save his wife Padmé's life was to help him destroy The Republic, Anakin was seduced to the dark side of the Force. As a Sith apprentice, Darth Vader nearly died at the hands of Obi-Wan. Darth Sidious saved Vader's life by encasing him in a mostly cybernetic body. In the end, Vader was forced to choose between saving the life of his son, Luke Skywalker, or serving Sidious. Vader chose to kill Sidious, thereby bringing balance to the Force and fulfilling the ancient Jedi prophecy.

HOW TO FOLD: DARTH VADER

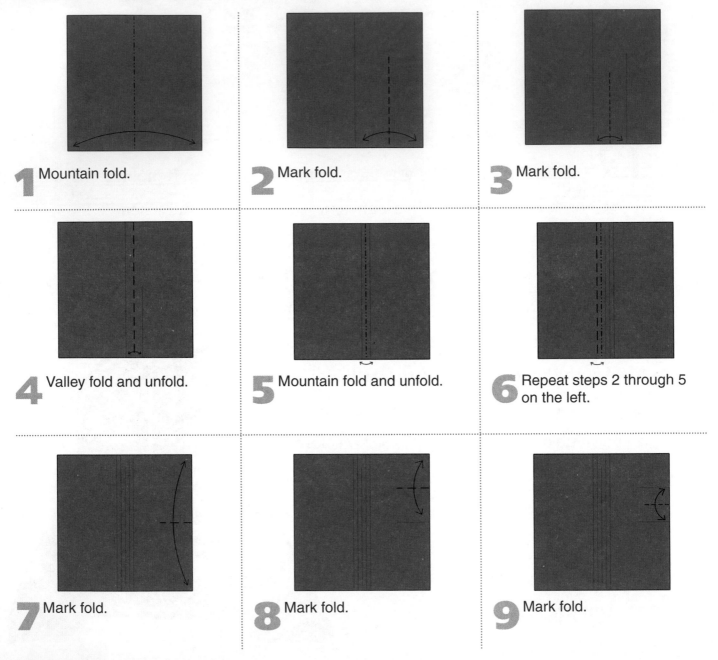

1 Mountain fold.

2 Mark fold.

3 Mark fold.

4 Valley fold and unfold.

5 Mountain fold and unfold.

6 Repeat steps 2 through 5 on the left.

7 Mark fold.

8 Mark fold.

9 Mark fold.

10 Valley fold and unfold.

11 Mountain fold and unfold.

12 Mountain fold and unfold.

13 Mark fold.

14 Mark fold.

15 Valley fold and unfold. Crease only from point A to point B.

16 Mountain fold.

17 Valley fold and unfold.

18 Valley fold from the intersection of the creases to the edge. Unfold.

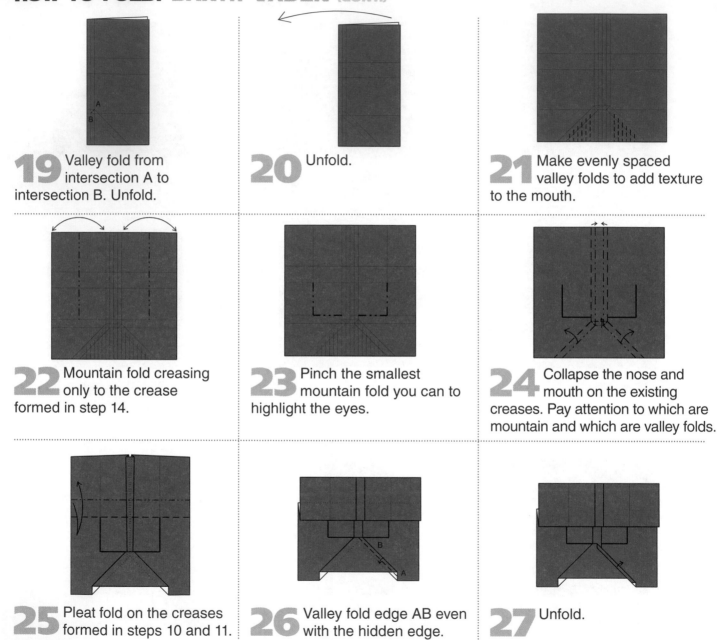

19 Valley fold from intersection A to intersection B. Unfold.

20 Unfold.

21 Make evenly spaced valley folds to add texture to the mouth.

22 Mountain fold creasing only to the crease formed in step 14.

23 Pinch the smallest mountain fold you can to highlight the eyes.

24 Collapse the nose and mouth on the existing creases. Pay attention to which are mountain and which are valley folds.

25 Pleat fold on the creases formed in steps 10 and 11.

26 Valley fold edge AB even with the hidden edge.

27 Unfold.

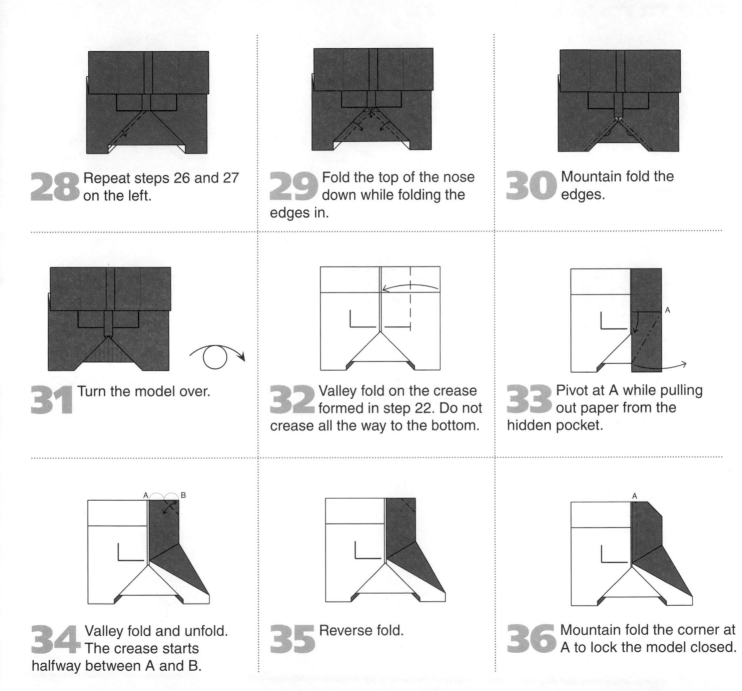

28 Repeat steps 26 and 27 on the left.

29 Fold the top of the nose down while folding the edges in.

30 Mountain fold the edges.

31 Turn the model over.

32 Valley fold on the crease formed in step 22. Do not crease all the way to the bottom.

33 Pivot at A while pulling out paper from the hidden pocket.

34 Valley fold and unfold. The crease starts halfway between A and B.

35 Reverse fold.

36 Mountain fold the corner at A to lock the model closed.

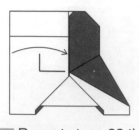

37 Repeat steps 32 through 36 on the left side.

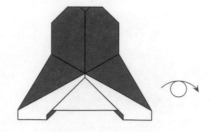

38 Turn the model over.

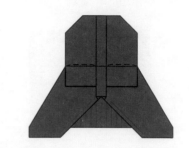

39 Valley fold the edges to form two crescent-shaped areas.

40 Crease the edges forward to suggest the edges of the helmet.

TEST YOUR STAR WARS IQ:

TRIVIA

1. What color was used for the designation of the Y-wing Squadron at Endor?
A. Yellow
B. Gold
C. Red

2. Who called R2-D2 a "nearsighted scrap pile"?
A. C-3PO
B. Han Solo
C. Lando Calrissian

3. How old was Queen Amidala during the Battle of Endor?
A. twelve
B. thirteen
C. fourteen

4. Who was a Padawan of Count Dooku?
A. Obi-Wan Kenobi
B. Luke Skywalker
C. Qui-Gon Jinn

5. Which of the following was NOT hidden in Jango Fett's armored suit?
A. Throwing knives
B. Dual pistols
C. A snare

6. What was the name of Lando Calrissian's chief administrative aid in Cloud City?
A. Kitster
B. Lobot
C. Dexter

ANSWERS: 1.B, 2.A, 3.C, 4.C, 5.A, 6.B

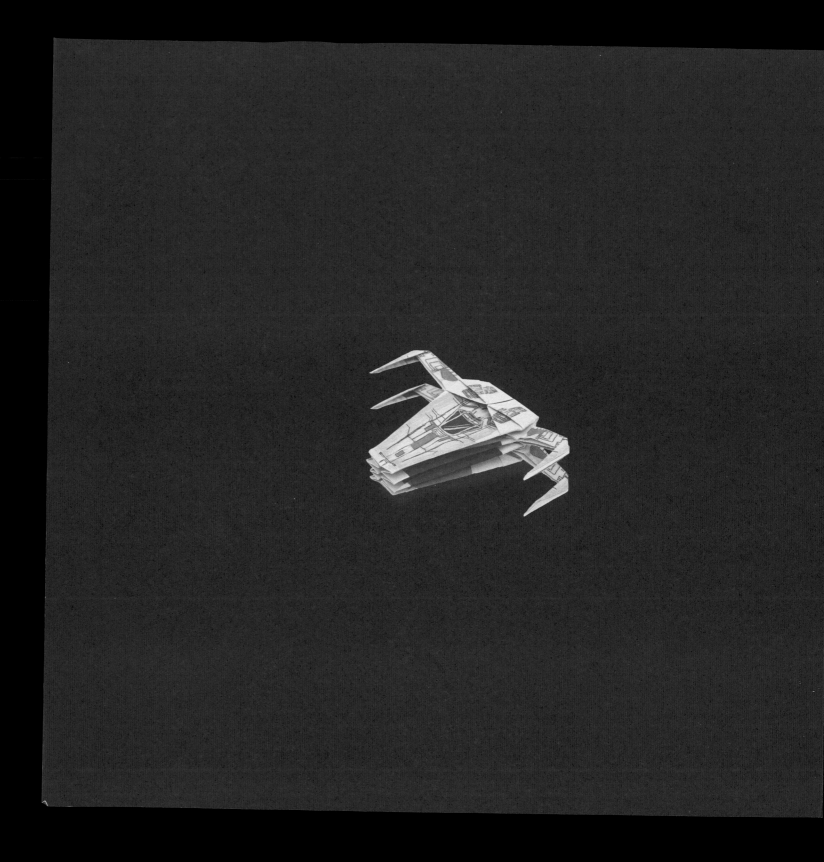